HUMAN EXPERIENCE

HUMAN EXPERIENCE

A STUDY OF ITS STRUCTURE

BY VISCOUNT HALDANE, *R.B.H.*

GREENWOOD PRESS, PUBLISHERS
WESTPORT, CONNECTICUT

Originally published in 1926 by John Murray, London

First Greenwood Reprinting 1970

Library of Congress Catalogue Card Number 75-98226

SBN 8371-3684-9

Printed in United States of America

PREFACE

WHAT this book aims at is a philosophical inquiry into the nature and meaning of human experience. The investigation is not directed to any particular variety of that experience, but to what the very existence of experience implies. This is a question that involves philosophy, and the method employed has therefore to be a philosophical one. The problem is not only more vital than we are apt, in our easy-going fashion, to take it to be, but it is also a further-reaching one. It forces us into asking what we mean by our minds, and into endeavouring to discover the relation of mind to the objective world. For we seem to have assumed, too hastily and perhaps unconsciously, that mind is a sort of thing of which our experience is a detachable activity or property. In this volume a different view is submitted for consideration.

There is nothing really strange or even new in the view so submitted. It is in principle as old as Plato and Aristotle and Plotinus. But from time to time questions of this sort have to be examined afresh, if

v

only that they may retain their vitality. There are those who may say that if the work of inquiry into the character of human experience had to be done over again it should have been done by one who was not on the verge of three score and ten. But experience is an obscure subject, despite our habitual employment of the word. A lifetime is required even for the reading of what has been said about it. Study is unavoidable, for I am unable to believe that the work of successive generations of great thinkers, who have concentrated effort on the significance of this "slippery" term, is likely to have left us wholly without some light. And more than the methods to which psychology is constrained to confine itself, even to-day, appears to be necessary before we can be confident of what the real problem is. We have to be clear as to the difficulties that confront us if we are to be assured of freedom from assumptions we are apt to make inadvertently, assumptions of which the greatest of our intellectual forefathers have told us, and which they have recorded for us.

But this book is no attempt at a history of these things. What it contains I have sought to work out in my own fashion.

Psychology and philosophy are to-day not divorceable; nor is there any lack of interest in either. The desire for philosophy has indeed assumed new forms. That the desire as fashioned in the forms of our period is widely diffused, the popular libraries and the publishers' lists show us. We are moved by the spirit of our time, and it seems clear that this spirit has not really done with philosophy. What shape philosophy will next assume no one can say. But its problems, as defined through the course of centuries that have passed, remain. The problems at least are still with us.

To show why this must be so, is one of the purposes of the book. It is intended to be an introduction to the study of the problem of philosophy as it stands, and not of its history. It is written to be read by those who are interested, but not of necessity much trained, in philosophical inquiry. The view of the character of reality set forth follows upon a prolonged study of the history of thought. Whether I have disentangled aright the true nature of experience must be judged of by others than myself. I would not have ventured to write had I not believed that the conclusions in these pages were at least in harmony with much that seems to have proved reliable in past endeavour in this region.

In the Preface there are two points which

may be specially mentioned. The inquiry has led to a somewhat closer investigation than has been usual of the significance of the Particular as a limiting factor in human experience. It is, in the pages which follow, distinguished sharply from what is Individual, a form from which it indeed appears to be a wholly distinct one. The other point is that experience manifests itself as of different grades or orders, and as at different levels. It contains logically different forms that thus enter into the real world and give to that world varying aspects.

The forms that so characterise the actual world, where they seem to determine its varying aspects, are founded in the ultimate nature of mind and are apparently ultimate phases in experience not capable of being reduced to anything outside mind itself. These fundamental forms fall into classes, which indicate degrees in the aspects of reality. Such classes embrace subordinate forms, such as causation, end, value, and many others, which in theory at least might conceivably be respectively exhibited as relations falling within some or other of the wider classes. Logic seems to point to this as natural. But the task of attempting to exhibit the subordinate conceptions systematically is not one which has ever been accomplished in a way that has commanded lasting assent, and reasons are offered in the pages that follow for thinking that the conditions in nature which restrict the capacity of human knowledge, its limitless range in abstract conceptions notwithstanding, render results so obtained unreliable. In any case such an investigation is unnecessary for the purposes of a study confined to first principles, and I have deliberately abstained from embarking on it.

The forms that are inherent in our experience thus mould the world which is disclosed in it, from standpoints that are independent but do not interfere with each other. The explanation is that in logical character they belong to different kinds of knowledge in its widest meaning. This principle of variety in the structure of knowledge is no novel one. It was enunciated definitely a good deal more than a century ago, but has had little attention bestowed on it.

Science seems to be to-day approaching more closely to philosophy, and philosophy appears to be seeking more and more for fresh materials to be drawn from science. I have referred to some extent to current physics and biology, but only in aspects which concern philosophy itself. It is not generally realised how much some of the most eminent authorities in science are now insisting on further reaching interpretations that are really more metaphysical than scientific, and are of wider scope than used to be held sufficient. It may be that some of these would rather let science take care of itself, but unfortunately the developing science of to-day will not leave its votaries in tranquillity. If anyone will turn to one of the most recent publications of a great contemporary mathematician, Hermann Weyl,[1] he will see how a thinker of this type is driven to seek for light from philosophy on the structure of experience.

As I have said, this inquiry is a philosophical one. But I have not spared myself in the effort to express the process and its results in language that may be intelligible even to those who have not studied philosophy. Whether I have succeeded in this I am not sure. For philosophy is a difficult subject, more difficult than is popularly supposed, and, like mathematics, it requires a technical training. Still, it should at least be not wholly impossible to describe its pathway in terms that will indicate something of its nature and direction to the general reader. The pathway of which an account is given in this book is only one among

[1] See his *Was ist Materie* (Berlin, Springer, 1924).

others. But what is here described has come to seem to me a satisfactory road to the goal sought for. It represents, at any rate, what I myself believe in, and its description contains a confession of faith.

The first four chapters of the book set out the broad outlook. Chapters V to XV inclusive are short chapters expository of the particular points that arise. The four concluding chapters sum up the results.

CONTENTS

CHAPTER I

INTRODUCTORY

What does Experience mean for the plain man ? Just the world we are aware of, as without and within us. But if our senses and organisms were different, these might be different, for we ourselves seem to exist and have our periods and stations within these worlds. Reasoning comes in and gives stability to an experience that is primarily only individual and personal, for the mind sets sensations in relations to itself. As in memory, intelligence is required for this. Experience seems only to have meaning and reality *for* mind. But this view has always been challenged. The latest illustration of the challenge is Professor Dewey's book on *Experience and Nature*. Analysis of this book. Experience for him goes far beyond knowledge, which is only a product evolved within it. It starts with being and having things. Cognitive property is not intrinsic. Things themselves teach us whether they are subjective or objective. Thought and reflection are realised only in a small class of existences. Experience cannot be distinguished into knowing and being, into mind and its objects. The line of demarcation is between blind action within nature and that which is directed and significant. The difference between means and end is only analytic. The end is continuous development of meaning. A larger conception of experience does not separate activity from meaning. Experience implies change in a connected series of events, and the end becomes the regulative means of control. Criticism by Professor Dewey of idealism and realism alike. Meaning is objective because it is a mode of natural interaction. We must not start with the idea of individuals with minds, or with a self with formal capacities. Philosophy is no more than criticism. But it is surely too much to ask us, as Professor Dewey does, to treat experience as actual apart from any moulding by knowledge. Every possible object in nature seems to have meaning only for

CONTENTS

CHAPTER II

THE CHARACTER OF EXPERIENCE

CHAPTER III

WHAT TRUTH MEANS IN SCIENCE AND IN ART

foundation, since the middle of last century, and the development in this century, of the physical doctrine of relativity, a doctrine which has great significance for the philosopher as well as for the mathematical physicist. The reasons for this. The doctrine contributes to the breaking down of the supposed sharp line of demarcation between the mind and its object. In what is individual the universals of reflection and the particularisms of sense seem to fall into unison   .   .   . pp. 36–57

CHAPTER IV

UNIVERSAL AND PARTICULAR

We mean by the real that which has significance beyond that of the vanishing instant. This is so in Art, in Science, and in common experience. We fix what we experience by generalising it. This implies some degree of reflection on our part and the use of general conceptions. Words always import these. They indicate that by abstraction from a vanishing element which we cannot seize or even interpret we have given a setting to what is individual and unique. But the real is not made up of thoughts. It implies the factor of the particular which thought cannot reach or define. Universal and particular are not separable as self-subsistent existences. They are merely aspects, distinguishable only logically, of the single reality, which is always concrete, and can only be broken up in thought by abstractions which are inadequate to it. The pure particularity in the actual we can never reach. If we even name it we have by an abstraction transformed it. It turns out to be merely a limiting conception, nothing actual in itself, yet essential as a moment logically as well as actually required in the constitution of a reality which is always individual   .   .   . pp. 58–74

CHAPTER V

KNOWLEDGE AND REALITY

Experience is no assemblage of isolated facts. Their inclusion in some sort of whole is always implied. Space and time. Relations involved as well as terms. But the abstractions of reflection are never exhaustive of reality. They have to start from what is individual. Experience itself is dynamic and not

CHAPTER VI

THE OBJECT-WORLD OF KNOWLEDGE

CHAPTER VII

THE SELF IN EXPERIENCE

It does more than feel, for it interprets its feelings. We invest the facts with their meaning and so with their existence. The self is thus the centre to which we refer our experience, and by which it is held together, and is there for us. The limitations of the dynamic capacity of the self arise from its having a station in the object-world of nature, and a definite situation there. For it depends on material belonging to the senses. To experience we thus come back, but to no mere external object. The object is no entity disseverable from the subject. It is only conceptually, in general terms, that the activity of the subject can be rendered. It is by what is called abstraction that we interpret it as self-contained. Science and art and religion contrasted.

CHAPTER VIII

HOW MEANING ENTERS INTO REALITY

The object-world no aggregate of bare particulars. The mind does much more than merely co-exist with it. They are not separate entities, for universals of thought are required in the constitution of the object. It is only for knowledge that it has meaning and reality, and these it gets by recognition in general conceptions. Illustration of this from what happens when a crowd listens to and observes an orator who addresses it. The factor of bare sensation on the part of each individual is private and for him exclusive and incommunicable. It is made actual and communicable only by being qualified by logical conceptions which are of a general nature, and which are identical in the case of every member of the crowd. It is so that the meeting is a real one. The abstractions of psychology. The true character of Induction. We do not copy, but pass from pictorial to functional expressions. Illustrations from science. Further analysis of the experiences of the crowd.

CHAPTER IX

INDIVIDUALITY IN EXPERIENCE

The actual is experience and experience is the actual. But both have varying levels. Experience is no static entity, but a process that is self-developing through reflection. None the less it is individual. Identity in interpretation at different levels is the key to the meaning of reality in the objects of knowledge. The dynamic character of experience. As mere isolated organisms we do not possess this, for the organism is relatively static, and thought is no property of the organism. The nature of the subject must be sought in that of knowledge. The dialectical character of knowledge, and how it reaches over its object. Art and religion. Their nature. The mere animal is not capable of them. The true function of education. The meaning of knowledge and its relation to experience.

CHAPTER X

THE FOUNDATION OF THE ACTUAL

The subject is the condition of there being a conceivable object, and it cannot be itself an object. It is rather a limiting conception towards which reflection impels us in our dissection of experience. But in reflection our own thinking is directly present in our minds, and it thus discloses its own character. Knowledge is no instrument and behind it we cannot get. It operates at levels and in conceptions that vary. It expresses itself in nature in a plurality of individual sentient organisms that are intelligent. Thus we are brought to the distinction of sense from thought. But thinking always enters into sense perception. The "I," as reflection leads us to it, is of the character of a universal, and the self is thus ultimately a single self, foundational to all individual selves, but manifesting itself in differing forms. The self, even as it occurs in experience, is more than the psychologist takes it to be. Ideally conceived it is not only beyond numerical distinction, but stretches over the whole universe, so that this falls within it. The principle of levels or degrees in knowledge accounts for the difficulties that apparently arise in this connection. But we can form no pictorial representation of the ultimate ideal, although it is intelligible ·to reflection. The method is more important than the result, and the symbols of art and religion help us, even though they can assist us to no direct vision of God.

CONTENTS

CHAPTER XI

THE POINT OF DEPARTURE

CHAPTER XII

MAN AND GOD

CHAPTER XIII

LEVELS IN KNOWLEDGE AND REALITY

The conceptions of reflection refer back to an " I " which is itself of a thinking or universal character. Thus conceptions enter into the reality of the " I " as an object to an extent that cannot be exhausted. The character of the identity of my neighbour, John Smith. In what his personality consists. Experience and the mind which experiences cannot be dissociated. The nature of knowledge. Its identity in subjects in knowledge, which on their object side are treated as numerically different only because of their aspects in nature, and so in time and space. These aspects mould the existence of the subject so far as it is indicated in the object-world. We find in experience different kinds of ideas. The reason is that the interpretation takes place in virtue of ideas of different orders, which therefore enter differently into the constitution of reality. But the interpretations do not come into collision, for they refer to what is a single object but at different levels. These are determined by the categories or logical conceptions which govern them.

CHAPTER XIV

KNOWLEDGE AND ITS LEVELS

More about what the identity of my neighbour means. Mind is expressed in it in objective form. What the soul of man is : personality expressed in bodily form. The value in this connection of the principle of levels in knowledge and reality. This is no *a priori* deduction, but a fact for observation. Citation of Hermann Weyl. The object-world contains the universe, and evolution takes place within its forms of time and space. But neither these last nor the object-world itself have significance apart from what is their other aspect, the subject *for* which they are, and which reaches over and is inseparable from them excepting by our abstraction. The idea of an ultimate reality.

CHAPTER XV

SOUL AND BODY

CHAPTER XVI

HUMAN PERSONALITY

CHAPTER XVII

THE STRUCTURE OF EXPERIENCE

CHAPTER XVIII

MAN AND DEATH

CHAPTER XIX

THE OUTCOME

CONTENTS

HUMAN EXPERIENCE

CHAPTER I

INTRODUCTORY

THE purpose of this book is to throw light on the real character of experience. The method employed for this purpose is not merely that which is familiar in psychology, but is the general method which is used in philosophy. For the solution of the problem raised turns out in the end to depend on an answer being found to a fundamental question with which psychology cannot deal, that of the ultimate character of mind itself, as distinguished from what seem to be its various appearances in nature. In dealing with such a question I do not think that psychological methods are by themselves sufficient. I am far from underrating their value for their legitimate sphere of inquiry. Psychology has in our days made enormous strides, and its command of new biological and other scientific knowledge has opened up prospects of still further advance. But this science tends, just like physics, to make characteristic abstractions which do not represent in their full scope the facts which press themselves upon us. Experience does not arise out of any merely mechanistic putting together of unconnected sensations. It seems rather to consist in what is more concrete and complex, but is broken up by the methods the psychologist employs into what are not facts but abstract descriptions of them, inasmuch as the supposed facts are severed from the system and activity to which they belong. Sensations, for example, as represented merely psychologically, tend to become such abstractions, for they are never experienced in isolation as we generally try to picture them by such methods as being. A complex perception comes first of all, growing with further experience in complexity. Psychological methods are apt to aim at analysing it, as it thus grows, into so-called simpler facts which appear to be something like fragments of the whole, and as mere fragments are deprived of their full character.

But the methods of the psychologist are none the less essential. They serve the inquiry into the character of experience as do those of the mathematician, by analogy professedly confining himself to an order in externality exclusive of secondary qualities, serve the physicist and the chemist who have to ascertain principles of a definite kind in what is relatively speaking less abstract, in that it includes more of what is the appearance to us of the world. In a similar way physics and chemistry are indispensable for the preliminary studies of biology, although they do not take cognisance of the ends, behaviour in unconscious fulfilment of which life seems to mean.

At the foundation of experience there lies system, not what is static, but the systematic activity of our minds. This we have to accept as present in our object-world, and we can neither explain it away nor finally resolve it into elements which are the creatures, whether we will or no, of a process in which of set purpose we shut out much of what is actually before us, notwithstanding that it in truth belongs to an indivisible system. What we really start from appears to be activity which never rests. Experience may be faint and undeveloped. But if it is really experience at all its resemblance is rather to a system of intelligence than to the externality that is characteristic of mechanism and in some degree of life. If this be so, the only footing on which our experience can be inquired into is one on which it is treated as analogous in character to what we find in our minds themselves. In my mind I include, not merely what is found in the object-world itself, but that *for* which an object-world is there, actually or possibly.

For many centuries the problem of the nature of mind has been the subject of scrutiny by what are popularly called philosophical methods. What this really means is that the starting-point, behind which such methods do not go, because they are forced to assume it as the starting-point, is the full world, without and within, as it presents itself for our minds. The task of philosophy has been to disentangle the significance of this world and to discover what is implied in its constitution. That philosophers have differed in their systems does not detract from the fact that for many hundreds of years some of the greatest intellects in history have been concentrated on the task. Despite their differences I believe that they have succeeded in disentangling for us a good deal, and that we cannot to-day neglect the results of a sequence of efforts which have been gigantic. These efforts have generally sought to bring to light tacit assumptions, which have obscured the obvious nature of reality, and have led mankind into a region in which the true character of our actual world has been resolved into unsatisfactory and inadequate abstractions.

The great problem of the ultimate character of the real remains as interesting to mankind as it ever was. It is the flood of unduly specialised inquiries into it that appears to have produced confusion and uncertainty about the possibility of any solution. And yet our belief in the necessities of a higher life than that of the mere animal demands the attempt at some sort of answer. That is why I have ventured to write, and it is in the hope that the book may not wholly fail to prove suggestive to those who are inquirers that it has been written.

What may be most convenient is to begin by endeavouring to ascertain what our human experience is taken by others to mean, and then to state as a background an opposite view of its significance. We must first ask what we have in our minds when we raise any question at all as to the structure we are aware of.

What do we mean when we speak of our experience? In the condition in which philosophy is to-day the question is an important one, and a precise answer is not easy. Yet much turns on the answer we give. For it is held throughout by most people that what fills our consciousness when we deal with what is actual is just our experience, and

that this experience alone is what is actual.
It seems to be essentially our starting-point,
and this statement serves not only as a
provisional reply to our question, but appears
to agree with the opinions of mankind generally. By our experience we mean the
world as it is before our minds, the world
that is without and also that is within us ;
a world that includes truth and beauty and
values and all that we are aware of. But if
this be true it does not carry us very far.
Our worlds and what we are aware of depend,
to some extent at least, on ourselves individually. If our organisms and our senses
were different our worlds might be different
also. A rabbit has a more contracted world,
and if there be an angel he may enjoy a
wider one.

Moreover, it is only a little of our worlds
that we can apprehend. We are conditioned
by our stations in nature, by our periods,
and by our histories. Directly we ask about
knowledge we find that we apprehend only
a fraction of nature, and for knowledge of
a wider scope we are dependent on indirect
methods of inference, where perception
through the senses ceases to be possible.
That does not limit our knowledge. We
ourselves exist within nature, and as parts
of it. Yet our intelligence is also a possible

object-world for us. Not through seeing
or hearing, or by touch or smell or taste, is
it a universe for us, but as the result of these
interpreted in reflection, a mode of knowledge which clothes what it encounters with
meanings, and, proceeding from meanings
to further meanings, is systematic and progressive, although indirect. Experience thus
includes meanings. Even apparently direct
perception never stands still or is confined
to itself. Reflection is always entering into
it, in some form however rudimentary. It
is through some degree of reflection on them
that we construct the significance of our
objects, and these objects, as we shall see,
do not appear to be real unless they are
significant. The barest feeling seems to require some significance if it is to be recognised
as actual. It is only if they are distinguished
that even the most rudimentary feelings can
be recognised as successive. It is in our
minds that sensations exclude each other,
and the more we try to get beyond what
seems insufficiently clear because of its very
simplicity, the more intelligence has to come
into play. Memory illustrates a way in
which successive experiences which become
present to mind are fashioned into a whole,
and, excepting in the activity of the mind
for which they have become successively

present, it is not apparent how such fashioning is intelligible. The barest ingredients of our experience seem to imply intelligence of some sort as containing and holding them in relation to each other. Apart from the presence, in some degree, of intelligence, they do not appear to possess even the vaguest meaning. If there is to be a world at all it looks as if it must signify what is present to some possible mind. It is only in mind and for it that perception has any meaning. But if the object in perception were not significant, and had no meaning at all for us, in what sense could we say that it existed ? To be and to be *for* mind as the subject to which experience presents itself, do not seem to be ideas that are truly distinguishable. There would be little difficulty in fastening on mind as that for which the world is there, and as the condition of its existence, were it not that mind, whatever else it consists in, itself appears in some sort as a limited object included within the world of nature.

What has been stated appears to be not very different from the ordinary man's view of the character of the world in which he lives. If it be true, then the part played by knowledge as the condition apart from which existence is meaningless appears to be a fundamental one. But this view has been challenged from time to time throughout the history of thought. It has been denied that it is legitimate to connect the existence of experience with its being *for* knowledge as its foundation. Knowledge has been declared to be a product evolved in the course of experience, and to have no place in its earlier and more rudimentary phases. This denial is not made only by pure realists. It is made by those who, not being realists, yet hold the distinction between idealism and realism to be an artificial and unnecessary one. There is thus an important view of the problem which confronts us that is different from the one which has been suggested, and it has to be explored.

It will be convenient to start our inquiry by stating this other view in a little detail, and by taking it in its most recent and thorough form. From the United States a new account of it has just come to us. We are apt to overlook the importance of the evolution beyond the Atlantic Ocean of fresh opinion about philosophy. The " seminal " teaching of the late William James stimulated in the New World a good deal that took time to shape itself. But now, not only in the form of the acute criticism which New Realism and Pragmatism have brought to bear but in other forms also,

American opinion has assumed a highly developed shape with which we have to reckon. I propose to select as the point of departure a book which seems to me likely to prove a characteristic challenge to certain of our usual standpoints in Great Britain.

In a volume published in 1925 Professor John Dewey, now of the Columbia University, has stated the argument against the theory of intelligence as being the foundation of experience with great thoroughness. Professor Dewey is one of the most distinguished of contemporary philosophers. He is known for his acuteness and originality both in the New World and in the Old, and his reputation as a thinker is very high all over the world. The book to which I refer is his *Experience and Nature*. The argument for his thesis is not likely to be found more thoroughly worked out by anyone else, and I think that it requires the careful attention of those who feel called on to ask what is the true character of experience. The book shows, moreover, mastery of the underlying principles of the sciences, and especially of the psychology of to-day.

Professor Dewey's principle is that there is no such difference in character, and no such line of logical demarcation, either in

fact or in theory of knowledge, as are sometimes supposed to exist between intelligence
and what is commonly called experience.
Subject and object are inseparable and they
fall within the same order of existence.
What we call knowledge is simply meaning,
and meaning itself is a stage in experience
to which its natural evolution gives rise.
Experience is thus, in the ultimate order of
existence, prior to knowledge, and the latter
is its product and not any condition preliminary to its reality. Knowledge is not
only no entity separate from nature, but it
disappears excepting as a result arising
causally from the interaction of events.

For Professor Dewey our experience is
prior to and extends beyond knowledge.
Things exist, and we *have* them in ways
other than that of knowing them, and their
existence is the precondition of reflection
and knowledge themselves. Their existence
is individual and unique, and is therefore
strictly speaking indescribable. They can
only be and be had, and finally be pointed
to reflectively. All cognitive experience must
start from and terminate in being and having
things in just such unique incomparable and
compelling ways. A theory of knowledge,
of how to know most perfectly, is indispensable. But the theory of knowledge has

been turned into a discussion of how we can know at all, and this error is due to failure to take the various phases of experienced things simply directly and impartially. It is caused by the bias of the intellectualist in favour of his own specialised professional experience. But there are not two kinds of knowledge whose objects have to be reconciled. There are only two dimensions of experienced things, one that of having them and the other that of knowing about them, so that we can again have them in more meaningful and secure ways. The real problem of knowledge is how to find out what for this purpose it is needful to know. The problem of knowledge in general is nonsense. For knowledge is itself one of the things that we empirically have. A man may doubt whether he has measles, because that is an intellectual term, a classification, but he cannot doubt what he empirically has, because that is an affair of existence. To know a quality as sensation is to have performed an act of complicated objective reference ; it is not to register an inherently given property. The epistemological sensationalist and the epistemological rationalist share the same error, belief that cognitive property is borne on the face and is intrinsic. Because empirical method is denotative it is truly realistic. Things are first acted towards and suffered ; and it is for the things themselves, as they are followed up, to tell us by their own traits whether they are subjective or objective. These terms, like physical and psychical, express classificatory discriminations, and there is no presumption of primacy on the side of the subjective. So with things that have been called subjective. Political institutions, the household, art, technologies, embodied objective events long before science and philosophy arose. Since nothing in nature is exclusively final, rationality is always means as well as end. The more it is asserted that thought and understanding are ends in themselves the more imperative it is that reflection should discover why they are realised only in a small and exclusive class of existing beings. The ulterior problem of thought is to make thought prevail in experience, not just the results of thought by imposing them on others, but the active process of thinking. The ultimate contradiction in the classic tradition is that while it made thought universal and necessary and the culminating good of nature, it was content to leave its distribution among men a thing of accident, dependent upon birth, economic and civil status. In so far as qualities of objects are found worthy of finality, the finding must eventuate in the arts which are of the character of search for meanings. Only thereby will thinking and knowing take their full place as events falling within natural processes, not only in their origin but also in their outcome.

The author of this iconoclastic book then proceeds to reconsider the whole character of experience. It is not susceptible of distinction into knowing and being, into mind and its object. The view which isolates knowledge and value from the remainder of the activity in which the nature of experience consists is but a survival of the notion that there are things which can exist and be known apart from active connection with other things. When man realises that he is within nature and a part of its interactions, he sees that the line to be drawn is not between action and thought, or action and appreciation, but between blind, slavish, meaningless action and that which is free, significant and directed. Knowledge, like the growth of a plant, or the movement of the earth, is thus a mode of interaction, but it is a mode which renders other modes luminous, important, valuable, capable of direction ; causes being translated into means and effects into consequences. All reason is thus method, not substance ; operative and not end in itself. It is no good outside the world of nature. The method of intelligence and of science is to recreate the casual goods of nature into intentional and conclusive goods of art, with meanings in which knowledge and values unite. And this is a process which takes place within nature itself and is not imposed on it from without. For the fresh meanings themselves fall within experience. Philosophy is in reality criticism. It has to appraise values by taking cognisance of their causes and consequences, and so expand and emancipate them. Consciousness is no separate realm of being, but is the manifest quality of existence when nature is most free and most active. When there are ends in view they are the plans which are *contemporaneously* operative in selecting and arranging materials. Every process of free art proves that the difference between means and end is analytic and formal, not material and chronological. The end is no terminal point, external to the conditions which have led up to it. It is the continually developing meaning of present tendencies. The idea that work, productive activity, signifies action carried on for merely extraneous ends, and the idea that happiness signifies surrender of mind to the thrills and excitations of the body, are one and the same idea. The first notion signifies the separation of activity from meaning, and the second marks the separation from meaning of receptivity. Both separations are inevitable so far as experience fails to be art. Both separations are inevitable when the regular, repetitious, and the novel and contingent, in nature fail to sustain and inform each other in a productive activity possessed of immanent and directly enjoyed meaning.

Experience, in the view of Professor Dewey, is never static but always dynamic, that is to say, it means change in a connected series of events. Every situation or field of consciousness is marked by initiation, direction or intent, and consequence or import. What is unique is not these traits, but the property of awareness or direction. Because of this property in our experience the initial stage is capable of being judged in the light of its probable course and consequence. There is anticipation. Each successive event, being a stage in a serial process, is both expectant and commemorative. The terminal outcome when anticipated becomes an end in view, a purpose to be used as a plan in shaping the course of events. Such an end is an intellectual and regulative means, degenerating into a reminiscence or dream unless employed as a plan within the state of affairs. But a natural end which occurs without the intervention of human art is a mere terminus or boundary. When we regard the object and qualities characteristic of conscious life as natural ends we are bound to go further and to regard all objects impartially as ends in the Aristotelian sense. We cannot pick or choose. When we do we are dealing with practical ends which are in one aspect natural, but are in another chosen by reflective choice, because they happen to be thought worthy. Such a classification is, of course, consoling to those who hold that they enjoy a privileged status. One of the reproaches against idealism is that by seeking to transform immediate objects into such as are better, it has claimed to exhibit a movement from merely apparent and phenomenal being to what is truly real. Idealism has thereby neglected the circumstance that thought and knowledge are histories. In that wonderful phenomenon of experience, communication, events are turned by us into objects, things with meanings, and the meanings are more amenable to management, more permanent, and more accommodating than events in their first estate. Meaning is a mode of social action with which we realise the ends of association. It signifies more than words.

Language is a relationship, not a particularity. Over this nominalism went wrong. Meaning is objective because it is a mode of natural interaction.

We must speak of individual minds and not of individuals with minds. We must not think that we can start with a self and then endow that self with a formal capacity of apprehending, devising, and believing. Otherwise any mind is open to entertain any thought or belief. To the simplest observation we bring habits, accepted meanings, and techniques. Subjective mind is a mode of natural existence in which objects undergo directed reconstitution. The ego has had its significance exaggerated in modern philosophy. The community of selves cannot be isolated from natural existence. Just because consciousness of meanings, or having ideas, imports in its intersection of the regular a certain contingency, light is thrown on the impossibility of deducing consciousness from physical laws. This impossibility is in truth only a conspicuous case of the general impossibility of deriving the contingent from the necessary, the uncertain from the certain. Unless there were something problematic, undecided, still going on, and as yet unfinished and indeterminate in nature, there could be no such events as perceptions,

When they insist on the certainty of the immediately or focally present or given, and seek here for immediately existential data on which to build, philosophers pass unwittingly from the substantial to the dialectical, and have substituted a general character for an immediate "this." The breach of continuity between nature, life, and man is gratuitous. " ' This,' [1] whatever *this* may be, always implies a system of meanings focussed at a point of stress, uncertainty, and need of regulation. It sums up history, and at the same time opens up a new page ; it is record and promise in one ; a fulfilment and an opportunity. It is a fruition of what has happened and a transitive agency of what is to happen.   It is a comment written by natural events on their own direction and tendency, and a surmise of whither they are leading. Every perception or awareness marks a ' this,' and every ' this ' being a consummation involves retention, and hence contains the capacity of remembering."   In its movement it is therefore conditioning of what is to come ; it presents the potentiality of foresight and prediction. The union of past and future with the present, manifest in every awareness of meanings, is a mystery only when con-

[1] See p. 352 of Prof. Dewey's book,

sciousness is gratuitously divided from nature, and when nature is denied temporal and historic quality. When consciousness is connected with nature the mystery becomes a luminous revelation of the operative inter-penetration in nature of the efficient and the fulfilling. . . . Knowledge is still regarded by most thinkers as direct grasp of ultimate reality, although the practice of knowing has been assimilated to the procedure of the useful arts—involving, that is to say, doing that manipulates and arranges natural energies. Personality, selfhood, subjectivity, are eventual functions that emerge with complexly organised interactions, organic and social.

I have endeavoured, thus briefly, to sum-marise Professor Dewey's argument, using as nearly as I could his own expressions. It is obvious that the conclusion is that know-ledge is just a phase of experience, and arises within and out of it by evolution. It follows that outside of any knowledge of it, outside of all consciousness, experience possesses an actuality of its own. It is something different from knowledge. Now this is an idea which scrutiny of the facts makes it difficult to accept. Professor Dewey does not fail to insist on it. "Consciousness," he says,[1] "an

[1] P. 308.

idea, is that phase of a system of meanings which at a given time is undergoing redirection, transitive transformation. The current idealistic conception of consciousness as a power which modifies events, is an inverted statement of this fact. To treat consciousness as a power accomplishing the change, is but another instance of the common philosophic fallacy of converting an eventual function into an antecedent force or cause. Consciousness *is* the meaning of events in the course of remaking ; its cause is only the fact that this is one of the ways in which nature goes on. In a proximate sense of causality, namely as a place in a series history, its causation is the need and demand for filling out what is indeterminate."

But if there be no object of which the existence as well as the character does not depend on reflective recognition in some form, this can hardly be so. No doubt the view expressed by Professor Dewey seems simple and easy. It puzzles people to be told that there is no world apart from knowledge for which it is there. That is because knowledge is in one aspect itself included in our world of objects. Mind is an object among those which are before us in nature. Our own minds fall together with and are conditioned by physical organisms. But mind, while an object in this aspect, appears to possess quite a different aspect, one in which it is the subject to which that object-world presents itself. As such it can hardly either be constrained by natural processes or be a mere thing within its object-world. Knowledge does not appear to be a property of a thing confronted by another thing independent of it, nor is it an event but rather that within which events fall. *We* do not create the world of events, because we are, in an aspect in which we have to regard ourselves, conditioned by space and time and their contents. But these are themselves devoid of meaning excepting for reflection, and it is accordingly difficult to see how they can ultimately precede and condition reflection itself. In this essential aspect mind may be subject, yet subject that has expression for us in an object form, although itself inherently such that it is much more than a form which proceeds from its making itself its own object.

In the rest of this book it will be necessary to try to see what meaning can be attached to this other idea of mind, when the character of experience is considered.

CHAPTER II

WHAT is experience? The experience of other persons I know only inferentially, so far as they stand for knowledge such as I am directly conscious of in myself. What I am directly conscious of is my individual experience. But this fact may not signify that the experience of which I am conscious as my own is simply a circumstance, in the world to which my organism belongs, that can be isolated by itself to the extent that other circumstances can be. For it is separable neither from myself nor from the world which is there for me. It is just myself as well as my world. It is the only fact that is self-contained and is immediately present to my mind—otherwise than by inference.

To say that what is actual, and that my experience of it as directly present in my mind are the same, seems at first sight to be difficult. For my world apparently extends both in time and in space far beyond myself. But the difficulty arises from an assumption which I tend to make. The world in which, in some sense, I undoubtedly exist is just

23

my world, a world not the less within which I find myself included. I am included in it as a finite being, as a being with a physical form that is the outcome of long processes of evolution. As such I easily take myself to be a sort of thing among the other things that are before my mind along with it. That is in substance what Professor Dewey seems to make of me.

But can this be the whole truth? What is the character of my experience when regarded with attention to the facts it exhibits? Surely that of systematic activity of my mind in bringing what it experiences within reflection! We can analyse the outcome of this process by well-recognised methods, and reduce it to the application of simple and limiting notions which do not take account of many features in what is actual. But when we do so we fall into abstractions which take us away from and not towards the fullness of what is apparently directly given. The systematic activity of experience goes beyond mere physical analysis. For it is only in and through it that there is any physical object-world at all before us. The activity of experience cannot be defined exhaustively in any set of physical or mental abstractions. It cannot be adequately described in mechanistic terms, or as a property of a thing. It rather resembles the activity of mind as we seem to be aware of it in our ordinary consciousness, and in such activity find it consists and has its being. And this is not the less so because what is present for us, and what alone appears to be directly found, is a mind which belongs to nature and is therefore finite.

But mind, even in its human form, has a quality that distinguishes it from other external objects. It has implicit in it actually an infinity of range and of forms, and the range of these forms appears implicit in every phase of its activity. Apart from mind as such we do not interpret and fix in even the crudest reflection the most rudimentary feeling. If such feeling is merely attributed by inference and not consciously experienced, we are in the region of what is only a feature of life as such. What biology and physics give us is what is so far inadequate that it does not reach the level of the individual experience in which mind knows itself as itself.

I mean by my actual experience just that which is mine as a particular individual in the world. In that world I appear however, as we shall see later on, not as a mere unintelligent thing, but as mind itself. I am not there for myself simply as an organism possessed of an activity or property which I call knowledge. I *am* knowledge, with a range and grades which include bare relations of externality of things to each other at one extreme, and values at the other. But I am this in individual form as a particular human being. It is for myself as cognisant that I am a living organism that does not merely live but is aware and knows. It is of course true that as such an intelligent organism I am descended from parents and from antecedent generations in the animal world. My origin as such an organism may have ultimately been a pair of germs, or even a single fissiparous germ. My history belongs to the past, and my present is conditioned by it, and by my position in time and space. Not the less it is for knowledge that the world, past and present, to which I belong is there and actual. From the standpoint of a theory of knowledge that world has significance and reality only as falling within knowledge. Ontology, the science of what is and how it has come about, is limited to the field of what I know. Ontology is therefore a science that is circumscribed by a wider science of meaning for mind. It is in this way itself a branch of epistemology. And that is why, as stated in the preface, I have preferred the methods of the metaphysician to those of the psychologist.

But the field of what is there and has meaning for mind is that of a mind limited by its restrictions and conditions as belonging, at least in one aspect, to nature, a nature which yet itself falls within the field of human knowledge. For the experience that is actual is only the experience of a being so limited. If knowledge were, as Professor Dewey would have it, no more than this, we should be face to face with a great difficulty. For knowledge would be merely something derivative, a property of a being whose dependence on it is inadequate as the foundation and explanation of our world. But it may turn out, when we look into the nature of knowledge, that it is to be interpreted as based on no physical analogy, and as neither a product of something else nor an instrument to be applied to it, and is of a nature that extends unlimitedly beyond itself. It may be that knowledge is what it is for the psychologist only with a restricted significance in which it is legitimate to take it as exhibiting an aspect that is actual, but yet implies what is fuller than that within which the everyday view of its nature falls, but as disclosing only a limited stage or degree in its character.

Whatever else we may think of the value of the classical investigation by which Kant revolutionised the dogmatism of our ideas of the character of experience, at least we may recognise that he taught us that we must not assume that experience is self-subsistent, with an existence apart from creative fashioning by mind. Obviously to some extent experience is contributed to by the character of the mind for which it is there. The experience of a horse is different from that of a man. But Kant's doctrine went much further than this. For him mind was *foundational*. It was not *a* mind or *our* mind, for these are ideas which we derive from a world already fashioned in forms of time and space, in which such separation in number gets its meaning. Mind for Kant, his synthetic activity, is indivisible and constitutive. Its work is of the nature of thinking, and it imposes on a raw material the forms of time and space within which it fashions its world creatively. Mind in this aspect is knowledge which becomes actual in the world which it constitutes, and presents itself in object form in that world as a finite self constructed by its own activity. Such activity is no thing or property of a thing. It is foundational and is implied in the world that is known, although, as its condition, it can never as such be presented as an object in that world.

This is a view wholly different from that of Professor Dewey, for whom mind or knowledge is never more than a product within the world of experience. For Kant meaning is no mere product. It enters into and is the very foundation of existence, which cannot be actual apart from it. When we inquire into the significance of the real, either for ourselves or for, say, a horse, we find this in knowledge which is more than individual, for it founds a world which minds have in common, and necessitates a wider conception than that of the number and events which appear within the field which it constructs.

We are brought thus to a doctrine of knowledge as immanent, and this we must not assume to be one we can cast aside merely because of the view presented to us by the author of *Experience and Nature*.

In this wider idea of knowledge our individual experience is our object-world, but is also more than this. For in another aspect it has for its foundation intelligence that is creative, as Kant taught. It is subject which can never as such present itself to itself in perception in the form of pure subject. It is the foundation of all that has significance in experience, but forms part of that experience only in so far as it has in our perception of it the aspect of one of its own objects. Thus it appears as conditioned by nature, with a period and a station, and so as finite.

Whether this view is a true one, only inquiry into the character of experience itself can determine. If experience, which we cannot in our perception of it go behind, discloses factors which seem its objects but must receive their places in the logical theory of its construction, it may be that while experience is our starting-point, it is a starting-point which can be made intelligible only if we recognise that it presupposes knowledge in a form that is more than merely individual. In other words, it may be that aspect of knowledge in which as thinking mind is implicit or immanent even when we treat it as an object in reflection.

One of the assumptions we tacitly make, in religion not less than in science, is that our experience exhibits a sharp distinction between ourselves and what is not ourselves. But reflection seems to force us to recognise that the self is more than a particular thing or event in the world. When we reflect the self is the source of fresh meaning in its object, and reaches over and includes and fashions it. It is, moreover, free to direct its reflection, not only over the whole universe, but to its own activity and to a free choice of paths. Our mental activity turns out to be more than mere passive awareness of a reality outside itself. Possible thought, although it may be abstract and expressed only in generalities, is limitless in its range and moulding power. It enters into the constitution of the meanings that are essential in the constitution of whatever is for us actual or even possible. As it is with the objective universe, which we treat as if there independently of our minds, so it is with what belongs to the nature of the mind itself. The self of which we are conscious implies on every occasion more than it seems at first to have disclosed to us. Were it not so, were knowledge an activity shut up within what the physiologist means by a nervous system, and with only what the mere stimulation of the senses brings to it, we could not know. The line of demarcation between subject and object cannot be a rigid one. Goethe was a profound observer. He had the insight of science as well as of genius. He knew completely neither the mathematics nor the metaphysics of his own day, and in consequence he made mistakes. But not the less on that account did he contribute greatly, by the insight which both his poetry and his scientific writings disclose, to the full comprehension and interpretation of facts. He saw that it was not only to without that we must look if we were to get light on the foundations of experience. He found it to be fashioned by mind, and that it was to what is immanent in mind that we must look, not only for the foundation of our objective finite experience within, but for the foundation of the outward reality of which that finite experience seems to be an outcome. It was this which seems to have been what he had before him when he wrote the well-known lines :

> Im Innern ist ein Universum auch,
> Daher der Völker löblicher Gebrauch
> Das jeglicher das Beste, was er kennt
> Er Gott, ja seinen Gott benennt.[1]

In the light of this belief in immanence Goethe interpreted both Nature without and Mind within. For him the self necessarily implied more than at first we take it to mean. This conclusion seems to accord, as we shall see later on, with what we find in the character of our minds when we divest ourselves of certain assumptions. It does not imply that we shall come face to face in our scrutiny of ourselves with any definable

[1] " Gott und Welt " (*Proemion*).

absolute. Absolutes are apt to turn out in
the end to have been only relatives, and
this Goethe seems also to have thought.[1]
On the other hand, we do not encounter in
the fact of knowledge a mere event in time
and space. For limited and purely relative
purposes knowledge can be distorted into
such an event, as if an activity dependent
on that of the physical organism, with a
period and place in the world of objects.
The self has a brain and nerves upon which
it seems to depend for its existence, and as
an object of and within our experience we
do not find it separable from its environment.

But the self has a significance that goes
beyond this. It is not only what lives but
it is conscious and has experience of its
objects and of itself as among them. It is
only as possibly presented in consciousness,
actual or imagined, that we can attach any
meaning to the object-world that, regarded
from another standpoint, appears so much
wider than the self that is included in it.
For that self knows as well as is known,
and is subject as much as it is object. Although an object in knowledge it is yet
devoid of meaning if, by our abstractions,
we seek to exclude from the fashioning of

[1] See his declaration to Margaret in the first part of his
Faust.

the actual the mind that knows. To be seems to involve and mean some form of knowledge, whatever beyond this may be involved. If we could conceive an object of experience, actual or imagined, which *meant* nothing at all, it could not *be* anything for us.

Thus consciousness is from the wider point of view not only passively sentient but actively intelligent. It is free and self-directing in its modes of reflection, and it is thus that we come to that order in our experience which we call mind and per-sonality. Indeed, the human organism, when interpreted in terms which extend beyond those of biology, even when still interpreted as our object in the form of a physical body, displays aspects which belong only to this fuller point of view, for the body acts in-telligently and expresses intelligence in its actions. Conduct of this kind implies no-thing short of intelligence as itself included within the object-world of nature with its many aspects and orders. The Behaviourist School think that mind means no more than the behaviour of the organism. They may be too narrow in their expression of this view, but at least they have drawn attention to what was at times neglected before they insisted on it, the presence of what is analogous to mind as among the facts of the external world. The New Realists have done what is not very different in the recognition they have made of universals as included in that world. The tendency of our time seems thus to be to break down the separation of the self from its object, and, by treating the latter as in its nature resembling the former, to supersede the controversy between idealism and realism. The gulf that was held to separate Within from Without seems to be a vanishing one. If we can find a way of progress towards the idea of an entirety to which both mind and matter belong, as no more than aspects distinguished in conventional habits of reflection, from the finality of which we can by analysis deliver ourselves, we shall have advanced some way towards the solution of the problem of the nature of the ultimately real. But in order to make progress we must endeavour to develop the problem itself in more detail.

CHAPTER III

WE fashion our ideas, not only of men and things but of gods, after our own images. Race, temperament, individuality, the influence of social surroundings, all of these move us in different ways to become anthropomorphic. The development of our history modifies the standards by which we decide, even as to what we regard as actual fact. The appearance of the starry heavens to a Greek two thousand years ago *meant* something different from what it means to-day. Its truth and reality had a significance different from what we attach to it now. Not only our reflections but even our perceptions are always in part influenced by the knowledge which is that of our own time, and this enters into and unconsciously moulds what we assume hastily to be passively received experience.

Moreover, modifications introduced into experience as time passes are not in every field so progressive as we suppose. For the standards of quality in an earlier period may be higher than those in one later. The

sense of beauty and the capacity for expressing form were greater with the ancient Greeks
than they were with later nations. The
religious sense of the inhabitants of Palestine
at the time of the birth of Christ was more
intense than later on. So also it was with
the pioneers of speculative learning in India,
the India of the Upanishads, of Buddhism,
of the Sankhaya and Yoga, and other high
systems of Hindu thought. When we bear
in mind that Indian philosophy arose mainly
out of a desire to regard religion as reality, and
only in a much less degree from any attempt
at exact speculative conceptions, it is remarkable that even in theoretic insight the level
attained in India became so early developed.

In our own case in the Western world
accurate quantitative knowledge, the knowledge which we sometimes prematurely term
exact, has been the dominating aim. It
depends, but not exclusively, on additions
to such results as have been wrested from
nature by observation and experiment and
tested by the measuring rod, the balance, and
the clock. These results, which are mainly
quantitative, we express in the form of
principles which, because they are general,
are abstract. They, therefore, never exhaust the riches of the concrete individuality
of the object-world. With literature and art

this is largely otherwise. The latter do not depend merely on general principles, although in their own fashion they tend to conform to them. It therefore does not disturb us that we do not surpass to-day Greek art or the religious consciousness of the early Christians. The quality of the images born of the spirit in the best periods of antiquity turns on the capacity of the mind to interpret from a standpoint the sufficiency of which has to be different from that of the man of science, a standpoint from which values which we cannot question, because they seem to us to be inherent and foundational, disclose to us what is, in imagery that is individual, the highest in art and religion as having meaning that is its own and of a different order from significance for science. Here the growth of value is independent of any process of addition. What is meant by progress in literature and art in each successive period has to be judgèd by tests of a wholly different nature from those in physics. We are concerned not with quantity but with quality. The values in literature and art, and in the history of religion also, do not seem to depend on the amount of work put together, but rather does the reality of what is accomplished show itself as indicative of the highest standards reached in the work done.

Truth thus appears to have different meanings in different kinds of human knowledge. And yet these meanings cannot be assumed to be of kinds wholly exclusive of each other. Perfection in reflective conception is one of the most important standards of truth in science, just as it is in art. The subject-matter to which this standard is applied must of course be different. Science is knowledge about facts, past, present, and future. Its conceptions must be adequate to the facts, and capable of describing them in the past and present, and of enabling us to predict them in the future. But the adequacy of conceptions, which go beyond the individual experiences by which they are tested in our observation and experiment, to some extent depends on quality. The mathematical and physical ideas of the Greeks are to-day inadequate just for this reason. Experience has shown that they fail both in range and in content. No doubt it is in large measure because the results of applying them have ceased to satisfy the tests of observation and experiment that we have rejected them. But it was not this failure alone that in itself suggested to us the ideas that are current to-day. Our modern ideas are the outcome of more penetrating reflection, stimulated

of course by shortcomings which experience
has demonstrated, but itself the creator of
its own conceptions. It was because of the
demands of experience, but not as the direct
teaching of experience, that Newton was
led to his discovery of the differential calculus.
He arrived indeed at a result not very different
from that to which Leibniz came about the
same time, but his reflection was impelled
towards that result along a different path.
Similarly, Einstein has evolved his new
mathematical methods not in the laboratory
but in his study, as the outcome of what
laboratory difficulties have impelled him towards as new methods required by thought
for dealing with them. It is here that
thought and not mere observation has given
its further meaning to science and has en-
larged the range of experience. Both observation and reflection have been required
and neither would have sufficed without the
other. What appears plain in these phases
of scientific knowledge is that quality is in
the end inseparable from quantity, and that
the former, though in a different fashion, is
as essential as it is in literature and art.
The mode of approach, the outlook, is different, but the ultimate standard of perfection in range of knowledge is not different.
    At a time when science and metaphysics

can no longer be wholly divorced in the thoroughgoing way that used to be thought possible, it is of importance to observe the illustration of the new attitude in a domain which is rapidly being recognised as one where both come in. Here we find fresh evidence in support of the principle that knowledge and its object, self and not-self, can no longer be scientifically treated as distinct entities, but must rather be looked on as no more than aspects within a larger entirety. In the progress of modern physics, and in the aid that this branch of science has derived from mathematical reflection, lies one of the most cogent illustrations of how thought penetrates into and moulds the meaning of experience. This of course concerns philosophy deeply. From observation and experiment in the field of physics inquirers have started, and by these they have been impelled to a deeper and more searching criticism of their general conceptions. The method has not been to avoid hypotheses. On the contrary, it has consisted in making hypotheses and then testing them closely in the light of facts observed. But the hypotheses that have stood this test have always gone far beyond any apparently direct individual experience, and to this no attempt has been made to limit them. It has been of the very quality of high mathematical science that they should not be so limited.

We see how, since the days of Galileo, there has been a succession of scientific conceptions of what experience really signifies, all of great importance, but of a value that has turned out to be relative and limited to particular periods. One after another of these conceptions has proved to be deficient in range, and has been reduced to being a mere milestone in the highway of scientific progress. These successive views have had their significance altered and their range extended, and this has not been merely or even mainly due to the direct experience for which they have shown themselves deficient. It has been by more thorough-going application of the wonderful power of thought in criticism that they have been superseded as century has succeeded century. Reflection has transformed the significance of things, eliminating ideas that have been superseded, and has even given things a new appearance for us. Newton invented his new instrument, the calculus, because the mathematical methods of his own period were no longer sufficient for the description of the phenomena of change which he had to investigate. The balance and the measur-

ing rod and the divisions of the clock had
proved by themselves insufficient for his
deepest problems, inasmuch as they could
not take full account of continuity, however
important they remained within the limits
where they could be used as tests. Rates
of change he could not adequately describe
without the new mathematical discovery
which was due to his genius. The progress
since Newton's time illustrates the way in
which reflection has further advanced in the
power to interpret and describe reality, and
in which it has coloured it. With him his
principle that a body undeflected in its
course by any external force pursues that
course in a straight line, implied that what
straightness meant was known. He took
space to be, just what the geometry of
Euclid assumed, an objective structure of
an unchanging kind in which things were
set, and in which the shortest distance
between two points was of the same nature
and quality everywhere, inasmuch as the
system was uniform throughout the universe.
No other conception of space would have
fitted into his own system. It was the same
with time. The events which occurred in it
were simultaneous or successive in the same
fashion and the same meaning for observers
everywhere. The disclosures made, as the

outcome of the tests of to-day, had not been reached so as to lead to difficulties in Newton's period. Such disclosures have made it necessary to ask the question whether space and time have the same character and qualities under all circumstances, or whether it is not necessary to recognise that the relations experienced in them are in important respects relative to the mind of the observer, so that there may be an indefinite variety of space and time relations the nature of which depends on the situation of the observer and on whether he is at rest or moving relatively to the objects he observes. This is no question of mathematics merely. It is one concerned with the general nature of our experience. Mathematical language is the most convenient and exact language in which to describe the modern standpoint. Without its aid the working out of the principle is impracticable. But the underlying ideas imply a theory of knowledge. A very eminent contemporary mathematician and physicist has recently declared that he could describe these ideas sufficiently without employing a single mathematical symbol, were it not for the fact that no publisher would print a book of the length required, nor would any reader be found to wade through it.

It is for the development of the results of the principle that mathematical methods become essential. For in mathematics we can operate with symbols in a way that carries us far beyond what we can actually experience, save in the relations between the symbols pictorially depicted. It is through this depiction that the symbols can be made the subject of experiments which lift us beyond what we can see or feel, in a fashion to which even the highest-power microscope affords no analogue.

Stated briefly, what the doctrine of physical Relativity tells us from the outlook of a theory of knowledge is this. Time and space are not, as even Kant took them to be, invariant forms which mind imposes as uniform on an object-world which it constructs on its own account. The relation of succession from such a standpoint is, said the Kantians, both necessary and uniform throughout the object-world, and so is that of coexistence in space so far as concerns the objects we call external. The forms of time and space must, just because they are forms unavoidably imposed, be uniform when we observe in them. Relativity physics rejects this idea as being inconsistent with observed facts. For the same reason it rejects Newton's conception of time and space as independent and objective frameworks of the experience which our object-world gives to us as merely passive recipients. For they can be, consistently with the results of observation, no more than relations, varying with differently situated observers, arising out of the interpretation of a basic though only partially formed experience foundational to that in which time and space relations arise, are brought into being, derivatively, and are distinguished. These derivative relations subsist only between the observer and what he observes, and they vary with his situation and with his condition as at rest or in motion of different kinds. They are derivatives arising from the analysis of what we are more directly aware of, derivatives which the effort to know exactly impels us to fashion. What we are actually directly aware of is no more than continuously changing events, unmeasured and unshaped. Properly speaking, such a field of basic change has no dimensions, but as time relations are as much constructed out of it as are those of space, it has been called a four-dimensional continuum.

Preliminary doubts as to the uniform character of the space in which things appear to lie had impressed themselves on the mind of a thinker hardly less great than Newton,

Carl Friedrich Gauss, towards the middle
of the nineteenth century. Later on there
was developed the view that space and time
also are neither uniform throughout the
universe, nor are self-contained entities.
They came to be looked on as relations
fashioned by abstraction from the characteristics of the deeper-lying world of experience, the simplicity of which had been
overlaid by reflection until it had been
resolved conceptually into two sets of derivatives supposed wrongly to be directly
apprehended. The real world of experience
thus came, though after the time of Gauss,
to be regarded as one in which what we
start from in our really initial experience is
not in space nor yet in time, taken as independent and self-subsisting relationships,
but is an assemblage of foundational events
in which space and time are not yet arti-
ficially separated, just because the source
of their distinguishing qualities exists in it
as undivided. If this be so, the inference
must be drawn that the quality of a space
system cannot be interpreted apart from
that of the time system with which it is
one in an experience which has not yet been
turned by reflection into two sets of abstractions. Lines which coincide and appear to
be of the same spatial character and length,

if they are observed in a particular time system, will not so appear to an observer with a different time system. Measurements made by the observer taking himself to be at rest on the earth will present themselves differently to an observer on the sun, which only relatively to him seems to be in motion. Indeed, this is no strange experience. We seem to see the sun going round the earth, whereas in a better view it is the earth that is going round the sun. It is the situation and motion of the observer that create the perplexity.

In a similar way we learn that events which are simultaneous in one time system may be observed in a different time system as successive. It depends on the changing time relation which a universe in which objects are constantly altering their courses and velocities presents to the observer from a particular place in it. If he is in Sirius he may find these relations quite different from such as the observer on the earth encounters. As we change our situations and pass from rest to motion with varying velocities, and consequently with varying curvatures, the spatial and temporal relations to us of our universe must change. The principle of relativity forces us to discard the common belief in the objective significance of simultaneity. Events may prove either simultaneous or not, according as observers are differently situated, and are or are not at rest.

If this be so it is not difficult to see why even inertial and gravitational motion have ceased to be separated or indeed distinguished at all by the relativity physics of to-day. There is no straight line in the old sense that is really experienced anywhere. In all cases the motion is curved in some fashion in accordance with the particular space relations which obtain. There is no necessity any more for regarding inertia and the sort of motion that is all that we really find in gravitation as manifestations of two different forces. They are simply abstractions of the same kind from the motion of bodies, and can be exhibited as equivalent by mathematical treatment of their characteristics. The universe being really one in which space and time are inseparable, each entering into the reality of the other, the final unit in observation is no longer a space line alone nor a time interval taken apart from its space system, but what is called a " world line," possessing what underlies the qualities of both and consisting in basic change of a temporal as well as a spatial character. Such a line cannot be measured on the footing of the old principles of Euclid, for these imply the self-subsistence of space and its independence of time. For the same reason the "world line" which constitutes the actual separation of two points in what is relatively at least foundational experience, has neither shape nor measurement. But it has ascertainable qualities nevertheless, which do not depend on shape or measurement, and yet enable mathematicians to describe it in a way that is strictly true whatever the character of the particular space-time system in which the world line is experienced. These qualities are called "invariant," that is, under all conditions of observation the same, and they enable mathematicians to find principles common to all space-time systems whatever they are. Such space-time systems vary by reason of the different significance of measurement and shape which they present, and measurement and shape have been extruded from the invariant characteristics of world lines, inasmuch as these do not admit of reliable estimation by the methods of everyday practice.

If we have, as of course in daily life we do, to measure and describe in ordinary terms, we can do it reliably by applying to what we ascertain by usual methods of observation, supplementing knowledge derived from study of the invariant properties which new mathematical reflection has discovered for us. The method is concerned rather with qualitative characters than with quantities in the ordinary sense, and it demonstrates how unavoidably reflection and inference have moulded apparently direct physical experience.

It is true that by science only ascertainable facts are to be regarded as possessing physical reality. But our view of the extent to which our own ideas have transformed facts which we supposed ourselves to perceive passively is always being modified. In science, as elsewhere, it may be said with force that "there is nothing either good or bad but thinking makes it so." The question always is what have we really observed directly, undebauched by unconscious assumptions. Events which seem to the observer on the earth to have occurred simultaneously, may not appear simultaneous in the system of reflection to which an observer on Sirius is compelled by his situation and movement. The way in which the sun seems to us here to be moving round our earth, whereas we are in truth moving round the sun, shows how easily relativity may enter into experience. If there may be an indefinite variety of space systems, in which space itself is not plane but curved in various forms, we must not assume that what we call parallel lines can never meet. Mathematics, with its infinite range of symbolic conceptions, can easily construct ideal conditions in which parallel lines may meet, not, it is true, in the space we picture to ourselves in our daily practical life on this earth, but in spaces which may well be ordinary space systems for observers whose conditions are different from what we take ours to be. Indeed, Einstein has offered us a variety of scientific demonstrations, based on experience of the movement of light between distant heavenly bodies, that the actual geometry of our real world cannot be Euclidean. The geometry of Euclid after all is based, not inductively on actual experience, but deductively on his axioms, a collection of abstract propositions about points, lines, planes, etc. Upon their strict truth depends the accuracy of the whole of his system. Now these axioms could not be proved within his system, because that system assumed and was founded on them at the outset. Nor could they be proved by experience, for experience, as Einstein and Gauss before him have pointed out, has never itself been so tested as to prove anything quite exactly. Our standards of measure-

ment for space as well as for time depend
ultimately on our observation of rays of
light, and are based on a velocity of light
which is not unlimited but is for practical
purposes limited and constant. Space being
relative as it seems to be, and what we observe
being mainly points where rays coincide,
we are not at liberty to assume that a ray
of light is the " straightest " thing there is.
It is all a question of whether we are at
rest or in motion, and whether space has a
curvature and what that curvature is. Geometry has to be kept in accord with physical
observation, of the general character of
which it is a theoretical statement about
the facts of experience, and no more. For
use by men and women here, whose individual
space-time systems vary only infinitesimally,
Euclidean geometry may be treated as sufficiently true for ordinary practice. But it is
otherwise when we are engaged in observa-
tions of bodies at immense distances or in
the study of enormous velocities even within
a small compass, such as those of the motions
of electrons. Then we have to see that we
have corrected observation that would otherwise mislead by taking care that our calcula-
tions are based on the standpoints which
the space-time systems involved require for
accurate description. For the regions in

which we can observe the very great and the very small in an experience which is never static have become enormously extended in different directions. With this extension our experience has disclosed qualitative aspects of which even the greatest among our forefathers never dreamt.

To sum up the result. If we seek for the most general and the simplest character in the world that confronts us, we seem to find that what is primary is an aggregate of events which we distinguish more or less imperfectly. The series of mere events belongs to a stage in experience earlier than that of objects. In these last, so far at least as the world external to us is concerned, events have become shaped and their relations to each other can be measured and described. But bare events, inward as well as outward, are formless excepting so far as we can just distinguish them. The basic relationship is that of mutual exclusion. They may overlap or pass into one another. But primarily they are isolated in one of two fashions. They either coexist while they shut themselves off from each other, or they shut themselves off from each other by being successive. Even in the " interval " relationships of the highly abstract tensor calculus this is so, and these relations are therefore basic in the experience of order in externality. It is only in the theory of knowledge that it is possible to inquire further into this basic condition.

But mutual exclusion in coexistence and in succession does not imply that we can measure the contents of this relationship as basic or describe its form as we do later on with relations in space and time. For the modern doctrine of physical Relativity teaches us that the resolutions into measurement and shape, although starting from the basic relationship between events, come themselves to vary with the situations and conditions of the observers, and are different according as they are in motion in reference to the events or objects they observe or are at rest. It is only at this later stage that the principles sought to be established by Einstein and Minkowski, and in one form earlier by Gauss, come in. Their teaching assumes the existence of a world of changing events as the foundation, with a quality in the intervals which is of an absolute nature, so far as physical science and fundamental geometry are concerned. That is what the tensor calculus brings us to. Spatial and temporal relations as measured and shaped it rules out, as being of a derivative order which is not final. If the theory of Re-

lativity is true it appears that the spatial
and temporal relations of developed experience accordingly belong to derivative
and subordinate orders, and not to those
primary orders in knowledge which we shall
afterwards have to discuss.

Here quality becomes important, the
quality of completeness in conception. But,
as already observed, it is not chiefly in
scientific conception that quality has its
distinctive function.   In art this function is
even more prominent. We read *Hamlet*,
or a great lyric, and we say to ourselves
that beyond the perfection of form which
we find giving meaning to what is said, it
is impossible for us to get even in imagination. That is because genius has fashioned
for us the expression of a great standard in
an individual form. The standard we recognise there is one different from that
involved by the scientific thinker. It is
the standard of a quality that has degrees,
but degrees that do not depend on addition
or subtraction, or on the interpretation of
order in externality. The standards in art
and in religion are concerned with what
the human mind accepts as most perfect,
but reaches in a fashion different from that
of the physicist. There seem to be canons
of value which bind us and which proclaim

to our minds their universal validity. And yet these canons are not of the nature of abstract propositions. We find their expression in forms that are wholly individual. If criticism tries to reduce that expression to abstract principles we find that it fails. The function of criticism seems to be no more than to guide our apprehension of quality that is before us in different degrees, but is before us in individual shapes. Such quality depends on no disconnected particulars. It claims validity of its kind for all places and for all periods. It is in this aspect of a character that seems to be bound up with the particular, and yet it enters into reality as much as do the universals of scientific reflection.

How is it that in art as in science universal and particular are thus brought into unison? How is it that all reality presents aspects which go beyond the circumstances of the observer and claim to be of a general nature? The solution of this question we must not try to avoid if we wish to make way towards truth.

The purpose of the chapter now ended has been to introduce the idea that it may turn out that the gulf between mind and its object, between the self and the not-self, is a gulf that is less definite than it is generally taken to be.

CHAPTER IV

UNIVERSAL AND PARTICULAR

In human experience we find a very marked division between the abstract and the concrete. General principles and the descriptions in which we embody them are abstract. They do not designate particular occurrences. What this means is a problem which confronted Hume at an early stage in his *Treatise of Human Nature*. He resolved the problem by declaring that, although all ideas are individual, a particular idea becomes general " when it is annexed to a general term ; that is to a term which from a customary conjunction has a relation to many other particular ideas, and readily recalls them in imagination." So far this appears to be true, but it leaves us with the question in what the generality of the term consists. What is it in a general idea that takes us beyond the significance of a mere particular ? A mere abstraction is unreal apart from some particular to which it gives expression. And it does not follow that it is nothing at all in the constitution of knowledge. Our experience appears to be of what is individual as distinguished from what is purely particular; individual inasmuch as it has a significance which it possesses only as expressing principles of some kind. A horse is such for us because we classify it under a species which a principle, however vaguely defined, determines. Such a principle is the result of reflection. Even if we say that as a universal it is our object, still it is no bare particular perception. A gnat in molesting it seems not to distinguish a horse, though a higher animal with some power of inference can.

What is individual, the actual unique fact different from every other in the universe, cannot be resolved either into what is merely general or into what is merely particular. These two factors are combined in it, and because experience is always of what is individual, the combination lies at the very basis of experience itself. If experience be knowledge this is not remarkable. Knowledge is systematic recognition which implies that its objects are fixed in thoughts. In itself thought, as we find it in ourselves, is concerned with what is general. That is, as we shall see, how we come to get at and interpret each other's thoughts. Into the particular feelings as such of our neighbours, we can never penetrate. It is only when sought after as objects of reflection that we come towards their ideas. Thought enters unlimitedly into the constitution of experience, even when that experience seems to be of what is only individual. It seems, in our experience of it, also to present itself at varying degrees or levels.

For experience, as we shall find, always implies such divergences in the kinds or levels of reflection which enter into its constitution and interpretation. There is but one experience, the world of the actual from which we start. But this experience discloses and seems to imply as essential in it degrees in its quality, degrees which are superficially taken to mean that the phases which embody them exist separately from and exclusively of each other. The working hypothesis that seems better is that these degrees stand for activities of knowledge belonging to different orders, and distinguished under different conceptions that belong to these orders. In our experience they can coexist and harmonise in what is an indivisible system.

We began to see in the third chapter how mind is essential to and moulds its object. The transforming power of reflection became apparent, and the sharp line between self and not-self appeared less definite. We cannot take as final distinctions, however apparently obvious, which are made only in an unreflecting way and from merely casual standpoints. But everywhere we seem to find that, though thought contributes to an extent to which it seems difficult to set a limit to the fashioning of things, still it does not *make* things. There is for us limited beings always an aspect which remains inexhaustible and indefinable in terms which are merely expressive of general conceptions. These attain their significance, as defining what are individual objects of experience, only when in union with that irreducible aspect, and we must set ourselves to the task of trying to ascertain the character of this aspect. We shall call it the " particular," in order to distinguish it from what is " individual " in experience. For to give significance even to the latter reflection is always required, although reflection does not by itself construct the individual objects of perception.

By our experience we mean what we find as making up the system of the object-world of which we are aware. Into that world there enter both what we call sensations or feelings and the interpretations in which we set them. What is actual must imply both, if our world is to have any meaning.

That world displays many forms, all of them ascertained under the conceptions we bring to bear on them. Mere sensation tells us nothing, for example, of atoms or molecules, which for feeling are not real. It is when what we feel has been brought into general and abstract form through reflection that we come to atoms and molecules, and to the order of events in externality. So with life. It requires distinctions made by thought to separate off, as experience teaches us to do, what is alive, because apparently characterised by self-control in its fulfilment of inherent ends, from what is merely mechanistic. In personality again, which involves the appearance of self-consciousness and also freedom of choice, we require for its recognition in our object-world yet another order of conceptions. In short, knowledge and its object alike depend on the appropriate conceptions concerned. And these conceptions, which we are compelled by the individual nature of our actual experience to bring to bear, give their reality for us, as well as their significance, to the objects so interpreted. Apart from the meanings they have for us these objects are not actual. Beauty is there for man, but it is not there for a dog.

What do we mean when we speak of what

is real or actual ?   In literature and art we seem to mean what has a significance larger than that of the mere passing perception ; something that uplifts what is transient out of its transience, and that has in that sense a character that is general or universal.   In science, even when it applies itself to an apparently direct and pure experience of changing events, we are seeking for truths that are to be general in order that they may be abiding.   In ordinary daily life even we try to name what we encounter, and to communicate its possession of general qualities through designations that are general.   All our words import what apply to resembling qualities in a multitude of different things.   Even if a dog barks he expresses to us an idea which is of general application, inasmuch as he and we interpret it alike in some fashion.

Now these generalities are all of them descriptions in which what is particular and so unique of its kind has a setting and is made intelligible as having a collective meaning.   If what is experienced were not intelligible it would have no meaning at all, and would be accordingly non-existent either for man or brute.   It would indeed be absolutely outside of any possible experience and so be unreal.   Unless we recognise a sound, by forming some conception of it however vague, it does not present itself as a sound. We have no notion of what sensation means unless it can be related to the observer himself or some other observer. It is thus that the real is experience, actual or possible. Nor have we any warrant for thinking that sensation, however in so-called direct experience it is apparently mere sensation, has any reality apart from some kind of recognition that brings it under conceptions and enables it to be described.

Still, this conclusion does not warrant a belief that it is conceptions that by themselves constitute reality. Thought does not, so far as our experience teaches us, make things, any more than things supposed to be self-subsistent apart from mind make thought. No universals, such as in all cases are our thoughts, have meaning excepting as expressed in particular applications. The actual is always unique and individual. We think in images even when the images most distinctly express qualities which have been brought to light as reflection discovers general principles in experience. A factor or logical moment of a particular nature is present although we cannot always segregate or define it. It is implied in the unique individuality of experience. It is there even when we think apparently most abstractedly. $x - y = 0$, and therefore $x = y$, seems an abstract piece of reasoning, even when we put the equation on paper. But we can only grasp it because x and y stand for actual concrete individual marks, unambiguous in our experience of them. We can operate with them only because they are such, and are therefore more than mere universals or conceptions. They are symbols which we interpret as conveying what is in a high degree general, but they have not the less to be actual individual images. And this is so because we cannot reason, nor develop the dynamic power of reflection through conceptions, apart from actual or imagined individual examples. But the aspect of the universal is what interests us, because it is that of which we are in search, and not the mere marks. The changes we effect in the marks are merely convenient methods which we adopt for the expression of reflection, and we care so little about them in themselves that we can perform this particular operation of reflection almost as conveniently by moving pieces of wood on a board. Not the less in each case do we require symbols to tell us what addition and subtraction signify.

It seems to be quite wrong to treat uni-

versal and particular as though they were
separate and self-subsistent factors in our
actual experience. They appear to be only
theoretically separable aspects of the actual
fact, what in logic are sometimes called
" moments," which we distinguish by reflection, on an actual that comprises both and
which is always individual, and not universal
but rather *unique* in the universe in its
subsistence in our perception by itself alone.
Our general conception of an individual
thing belongs indeed only to our thinking
about it ; it is a notion formed in a process
of abstraction. Nevertheless it is an essential
aspect in knowledge. It is formed necessarily, because all knowledge is of the nature
of abstraction from individual experience, and
excludes bare particularity. It is by putting
out of mind what is irrelevant to the kind of
knowledge we are seeking in what is before
us, that we classify, and assign order and
meaning in our daily lives. But we nevertheless experience neither classes nor orders
excepting as expressed in their members.

With the equally essential moment of
the particular it is different. We can never
present to ourselves even in thought the
particular as such. It is only negatively,
as a limit which human reflection in universals can never reach, that we can even

refer to it. For when we try to define it affirmatively we always find ourselves giving it a defined and general character, and are describing it in terms which take us beyond the true vanishing particular. Yet it is only by transforming our general notions into something that is concrete and individual that we can reach reality or give to fact as such a meaning. Particularity is a moment or factor which is logically as well as actually essential in the constitution of reality, for a mind which finds itself as an object within its own world, even if the reality be no more than an image in the mind. That is the difficulty of ordinary subjective idealism.

But this particular moment is not the less no self-subsistent entity. It is only in its setting in universals, which transform it by giving it a character capable of description, that it is real for the observer or in itself, and the reality thus constituted is neither merely particular nor merely universal. The two factors are actual only in a union from which they are extricable solely by abstractions which deprive them of all actual character beyond what they possess in their union. The concrete and unique fact which the union expresses has both aspects, but the factors stand only for aspects of what is single and impartible, and they have no existence in independence. The attempt to run the particular as such to earth ends and always must end in failure. For it is a will-o'-the-wisp and not even so much as that. It is a limiting idea which we approach only asymptotically, that is to say, an idea with which in our perception we can never come up. It has its function solely as a necessary moment in the fundamental reality from which indeed thought, always abstractive, can by definition separate out what is general but seeks in vain to define what is implied as particular. The fundamentally real is what we find in experience, and its form can be only that which we call individual.

The character we find in works of art seems to bear out this view. I will cite a redoubtable witness. The citation is from the little book which the poet Swinburne wrote about the sisters Brontë. Of Charlotte's genius for making the figures she describes stand out and live, as in the instance of Rochester, Swinburne says that this gift is the rarest of all faculties of imagination, when applied to actual character. " It is a quality," he adds, " as hard to define as impossible to mistake." Art, Swinburne seems to say, is essentially directed to what is unique and individual.

But it must not be assumed that the work of the artist is on that account independent of aid by reflection. As an acute French critic, Scherer, has observed in his essay on George Eliot : " Among all the contradictions of which life is made up, there is none more constant than this—that there is no great art without philosophy, and that there is no more dangerous enemy of art than reflection." Bearing in mind the fashions in which Dante, Shakespeare, and Goethe, among others, have surmounted the difficulty to which Scherer refers, we need not be deterred from recognising universals as entering in some shape, even in art, into the individual forms of experience.

Every object in our experience, even when it is most shot through by reflection, is in ultimate analysis, as we have seen, individual in character. It is not only concrete, but it is unique and stands for itself alone. It is by its nature self-contained, and distinct from every other object in the world. There may be an unlimited number of resembling objects, but each of these turns out, when apprehended without distortion by abstraction, to have its own unique individuality, and to be self-contained and sole, like whatever we first started from. It is so in experience in every form, in art, in religion, and in science. Even in our relations to the other sex we fall in love with persons and not with qualities.

And yet, though individual and self-contained, each object of experience seems to possess the nature of what has been called the " concrete universal." That is to say, into its nature there enter aspects and qualities that are general and that can only be recognised and described in conceptions that apply equally and without restriction to an indefinite number of other objects. These conceptions as universals are required for the recognition and description of the original object. But should we desire the description to be unambiguous and to refer us to the object as unique as different from every other in the universe, there is another factor demanded if the object or image is to appear real, and if logic is to be satisfied. It is the factor of a demonstrative particularity which can be indicated only by shutting out all that is capable of description, and is yet implied in what is individual and actual as even imagined. It has just been shown how particular and universal are not things separable in the real, but are the moments in individuality which the logic of the real requires. What we encounter throughout our experience is that universal and particular have meaning for us merely as united in an individual form. The daisy on the turf has an infinity of qualities which are equally those of all other daisies. Such qualities we can name in language of general application. And yet what we look at and point to is not the less on that account a particular daisy. What makes it so we cannot explain in general language. The individual of experience is a final fact. Not the less all explanation is true only of possible members of some class. Even if we just point a finger and touch the flower this identification can be expressed only in terms that are general. The daisy is this one, here and now. But when we move, these identifications by touch will apply in the case of the neighbouring plant, because this has become here and now in place of being there and then. Such distinctions as these are can be made out only in adjectives which apply to a number of daisies. " Here " and " now " are thus themselves universals. No doubt the daisy we first saw was at such and such a distance from our hand at a particular instant. But then so may be the neighbouring daisy if we turn round and assume a similar position. In what does the particular existence of either daisy consist ? Surely in this that it is just that unique and individual object of experience. But the uniqueness appears to involve more than qualities by which no one daisy was really distinguishable from the other. It implies that the experience in which the reality of the daisy consisted for us was more than merely general knowledge ; it was an experience standing by itself in the universe. It was unique, not in virtue of properties, collected from our experience only through general conceptions, but in virtue of something more required by the object in order to make it actual, if it was to be present to us as just this unique and unambiguously individual flower, distinct from all the rest of existence. What this something more is we cannot define affirmatively, for whenever we try to do so we find ourselves introducing notions of general application, which, being of the nature, not of what we are passively aware of, but of reasoning, are not admissible. We can only indicate the aspect that does not so come to us negatively, accepting it as a factor which eludes and must continue to elude our reasoning, and which is yet essential, because without it experience is not of what is actual. The logically necessary moment of particularity is thus, so far as we seek to get at a conception of it, a conception merely limiting to the process of reflection, a

limit which we can no more picture to ourselves than we can a limit in an algebraic
series. Yet just as the limit in algebra may
be required for the adequate symbolic representation of the series, so here in our common
experience the particular is indicated as required in order to impart to it unity. For
our experience is always passing beyond its
apparent fixity in thought; it is always
dynamic and never at rest. It is ever extend-
ing itself beyond what it is at the instant.

The actuality and unity which belong to
the individuality of the unique daisy are
therefore what we cannot define by trying
to resolve that individuality into an unending
series of general qualities lying beyond apparently immediate appearance. Outside the
actual there is nothing immediate. We are
driven back in our explanations on inference
which always remains inference. Experience,
including such inference and thus understood,
is the basic form of our knowledge. Such
knowledge, however, cannot be exclusively
abstract. It starts from and it refers back
to experience, the ultimate character of
which is individuality, the universal with
an aspect in which it is in fact concrete, and
implies the aspect of the particular. Yet
that experience is also of the nature of its
universals, because apart from what is

general it would not only be incapable of description, but would be wholly without meaning, and accordingly without existence. Our inferences about what is individual enlarge its meaning and so develop the significance of its individuality.

What are popularly called idealism and realism seem both to be one-sided, and insufficient for the explanation of the actual. The actual is the experience which involves both thinking and feeling for minds constituted as ours are constituted.

CHAPTER V

KNOWLEDGE AND REALITY

IN the chapters which follow, up to the seventeenth, we shall seek to illustrate the general principles laid down in the four preceding chapters. It will mean dealing with special applications of these principles, which have now to be made applicable to particular problems. This will involve from time to time some repetition. But the reader may find it to be no mere repetition, in so far as it brings out the further significance in detail of the broad view of human experience here laid down. It is necessary to make plain by examples how that experience is constituted through reflection, building particularism into systematic form through the universals which arise in thought alone, although they become real only in individual form.

Let us start from the notion of a group of things. What does the notion of a group imply?

If we could observe objects as completely isolated from each other, and so limit our knowledge as to be aware only of each in itself alone, shutting out all consciousness of any relation between the objects, we should not get to the notion of a group. We should not even present to ourselves a succession of isolated awarenesses occurring one after the other, and the idea of a group, say, of four, or of anything resembling it, would have no meaning for us. For four implies a definite general conception descriptive of relationship. It may cover and be constituted by different arrangements of its content, one and three, for example, or two and two. But in itself four is an idea so far as it goes complete in itself, a number of many applications and having general properties that are all its own, such as that of being the square of two. It is an idea that involves what is general and not individual, save when an individual sign of four, or an arithmetical symbol for it, the number 4, is fashioned and made part of actual experience. It is so that we get to the aspect of the particular which is inherent in every individual object of experience, and this enables us to pick out and operate with 4 as a symbol or image. But what gives the object thus fashioned its importance for us is the relations which in our abstract reflection we attribute to it in order in quantity. So far as it suggests these to reflection it

suggests them as of general application. It
is this significance and the implications which
are unravelled in it by thought that make
the sign what it is. Its merely individual
form imports little else than a sign for us.
It is the significance and implications that
are the source of all notions about the number
four and that even enlarge its meaning for
us. Reflection is never merely static.

What is true of our experience of number
is true of all experience. It is no incoherent
assemblage of isolated or self-subsistent or
mutually exclusive particular facts. Inclusion in some whole is always implied.
There are no parts which stand by themselves.
If by inference we get at the notion of what
we cannot see, say an atom, the inference
takes us further. For we are forced to
recognise that even if we could see the atom
with a microscope we should become aware
that it was not only not isolated but was no
real atom, because we should go on to divide
the space occupied by it into spaces occupied
by yet smaller bodies. On the other hand
we could not identify the original atom
excepting as related to the contents of a
larger space in which it was included, and
so to other possible atoms in that space.
The smallest conceivable terms into which
we resolve experience thus imply relations

to other terms, and the relations belong
to a larger whole just as much as do the
related terms themselves. What are related
and the relations are significant only for
reflection of some kind, because they are
capable of being recognised and identified
only in so far as they express notions which
are of general application. What is true
of space is also true of time. The present
instant is real only as distinguished from
past and future instants, the " has been "
and the " is to be," and it is dependent on
these for the meaning which makes it a real
present instant to us. So far as we apprehend it, it implies a past and a future between
which it tends to become a bare division,
finally without duration and reached only
by abstract thought. Here also reality is
inherently relational whatever it may be
besides.

What are in this respect characteristic of
experience are terms and the relations which
make them what they are. Still, we require
more than the abstractions of reflection to
give us these. Universals are essential, but
they cannot become actual in our awareness
apart from the particularity which they fix
and to which they impart meaning, and from
which they are again abstracted in reflection.
What is actual is individual ; a whole which

we view in aspects that are universal, but aspects which we get by extruding so far as we can what we try to make particular and evanescent. It is only in thought that we can fix experience or break up the individual and resolve it into its logical factors. The aspect of the whole which the individual always presents cannot be detached as independently real from the details in which it is expressed.

But how is the combination possible which is characteristic of what is actual only as an entirety ? Certainly not as the outcome of any process like addition or subtraction. For such processes presuppose individual objects as already there in relation to each other. An entirety is implied, as in number, before a group of such objects can be apprehended. The explanation of such apprehension must be sought from a wider standpoint than one which reaches no further than to particular objects. In experience relations are always either developing themselves anew or are disappearing. They belong to an inclusive process which is dynamic and which never comes to rest. It is only derivatively and by abstraction that we get to any idea of rest. That was why Heraclitus long ago declared that all things are in a state of flux, and that is why no one since has been able effectively to contradict him.

Now we find this feature of self-creation and change evident everywhere in our experience. It is so familiar there that on this account some people have come to speak of experience as consisting in a process that is *dialectical*. They mean that our experience is no static or fixed assemblage of disconnected units, but that its essence lies in transition from one idea to another, and that its aspects involve each other, even when they are so apparently different as are spatial togetherness and temporal succession, or even existence and non-existence. The aspects which experience presents seem to belong everywhere to a larger whole. Space and time are now, as we have already seen, looked on by many physicists as being no independent and uniform objective relations of things such as Newton took them to be, but rather as dependent on relations of order in the field of observation that contains the observer and what he observes. Time refers us to space, in terms of which alone we can measure it, as on the dials of our watches, and analogously space means the coincidences of events in particular time systems. Their relations as they occur in our experience are conceived as being neither

uniform nor static.   They depend on whether
the observer is to be treated as at rest or
in motion of different kinds, curvilinear or
rectilinear. The outcome of acts of interpretation, they have the form of abstractions
from what is really fundamental in our
experience of the object-world, a state of
things in which we are aware of the real as
time-like as well as space-like, and proceed
by reflection which is abstract to divorce a
temporal order from a spatial. It is only
when this divorce has been made that we
reach the derived aspects, made what they
are by reflection from differing but relative
points of view, in which it becomes possible
to introduce the secondary ideas of measurement and of shape. The primary space-time
basis from which the start is sought to be
made is to-day sometimes called the continuum, and has become the subject of a
science by which its qualities may be ascertained. But these fundamental qualities
must be ascertained in forms in which they
are invariant for all systems of measurement ;
they exclude relativity to an observer, for
measurement and shape are foreign to their
subject-matter, and belong only to a secondary
stage. The world of observation is a world
of change. But even change is not found in
continuous form. Continuity is itself an

abstraction, unintelligible apart from discontinuity or discretion. It is therefore not surprising that modern research should have found itself face to face with a newly-discovered phase or fact in experience, the fact that action, that is energy interpreted as characterised by a basis in time as much as in space, and by the change which it exhibits, discloses activity in the form of discontinuous *quanta*, themselves presumably defined, and found only in abstraction from aspects of continuity.

Here, as in other regards, experience presents itself in forms the characteristic of which is terms vanishing into relations and relations vanishing into terms, neither terms nor relations turning out to be self-contained entities. The field of experience is just the process and theatre of this movement. In order that its actual nature may be accounted for, we require a foundation other than the mere abstractions in virtue of which there is suggested to us the idea of a static object-world confronting us, and subsisting independently of the participation in its constitution of our intelligence. The dialectic of experience implies more than quantitative order in externality. Its activity seems to be rather of a nature akin to what we are conscious of in the activity of intelligence itself, which is present as an entirety implied in every particular application of its activity. It is grasped as it is in our consciousness of it that our world has that unity in difference that makes it a whole for us.

Such a view may not be consistent with the old ideas of fixed frameworks, such as space and time were supposed to be, in which objects exist unaffected by our perception of them. The new view, leading us as it does to perpetually changing experience itself as the basis of reality, does not admit of our assuming the validity of those classical axioms of Euclid the exact truth of which no experience has established. It is more in accord with the conception of the field of experience as marked out by the intersection of " world-lines," as much time-like as space-like, and intersecting in points which we are aware of as positions in a field where all is in a state of change. In the language of modern mathematical physicists all really ascertainable facts are qualitative relations between the coincidences of such world-points; relations which do not vary in space-time systems that in other respects themselves alter with change in the situation and movement of the observer. Here we come, at least provisionally, to a limit to the operation of the principle of physical relativity, and to an apparently unaltering physical basis for reality. It is in descriptions of quality rather than of shape and measurement that the account of this invariant basis must be rendered. But if we recognise the relativity of shape and measurement, and scrutinise its validity in the light which the idea of their invariant basis throws on them, we are delivered from difficulties in our apparently direct observation that seemed otherwise to be perplexing. For mind turns out to have moulded the shape and measurement of its objects in a way of which the earlier physicists did not dream, and the supposed objectivity of the world has been brought within narrower limits than they knew of.

In the contemplation of living objects, again, we are being forced to make analogous admissions about the inadequate explanation of facts to which the mechanistic ideas of the old biologists confined us. Here also the twentieth century is witnessing the introduction of change. Conceding all that the principles of evolution and of natural selection have to tell us, as well as the laboratory results of biochemistry, there still remains a great residuum that merely mechanical conceptions do not render. The reproduction of the individual members of a species

and their inheritance of identical and specific
form and function, seem wholly unintelligible
unless we resort to a new view of life as
consisting in unconscious fulfilment of ends.
Life in this view operates as the whole in
which its living members mould themselves
as if influenced not by causes acting from
without, but through ends which are present
in the members and are realised in their
changes. It is here again no question of
action at a distance in space or time, but one
of *behaviour* in the immediate present. The
principle of rational order as prevalent on
which probability rests excludes the idea
that the reproduction of the individual descendants of one or two organisms, where
the descendants strictly resemble each other
in organisation and are yet of myriad num-
bers, can be due to mechanical causes, by
necessity separated in time and space from
their effects, and of the non-teleological nature
which is all that physics and chemistry can
admit. The rational view and that to which
observation points is one of the processes
as signifying the direct and immediately
present self-realisation of ends beyond space
and time separations and immediately operative. The same thing is apparent in the
phenomena of heredity. The continuity there
witnessed can hardly be the accident of

accidents. It is surely the outcome of influences that are general as well as directly dominant. Only the conception of ends realising themselves in forms and functions through life from its very beginning can explain this continuity.

But such ends, manifest as they are in phenomena external to the observer, are by no means necessarily to be identified with conscious purposes. When we come to what is a yet higher phase of experience, what we are aware of is mind itself, or purpose characterised by free choice in which intelligence as a whole may be implied in its integrity. There seem indeed to be exemplified intermediate stages between the mere self-realisation of ends apart from consciousness and fully intelligent choice. It is not necessary to suppose that the bee or the wasp has considered its path in concepts of free reflection before it can find its way to its hole unerringly from a distance. Instinct, with its unconscious selection, is a surer guide than logical effort. In the former the species itself seems to be dominated by ends operating generally, while in the latter there is room for individual freedom in choice, and therefore for error. Mistake is the badge of freedom. Mind, in this respect resembling both unconsciously self-realising ends and instinct, is for ever freely fashioning wholes out of details. But for the mind that depends on senses conditioned by an organism the details must remain contingent and uncertain. As expressed in us mind is thus conditioned by the organism and is therefore finite. Its grasp can never be perfect, and the contingency of the details can never be wholly overcome.

What seems clear is that the relations between events, separated from each other in their order in externality, cannot express such relations as those between ends and the behaviour which they control in what is living or as those between thinking and volition. More than differential equations, or even tensor equations, which are founded on the principle of order in externality as final, are required for the expression of these other relations. In different words, a fresh set of conceptions of a further grade in knowledge are requisite if the nature of certain phases of experience is to be described.

We must try to ascertain what this fact of our experience implies.

CHAPTER VI

THE OBJECT-WORLD OF KNOWLEDGE

OUR world as it is before us discloses, as
we have now seen, much more than relations
in space and time, or even than ends realising
themselves in beings that merely live unconsciously. It presents to us self-conscious
mind in object form. I see other people
around me and I recognise in them selves
like my own self. These I perceive in my
direct experience just as I perceive myself.
Such perception is, not of generalities, but
of those objects in my actual experience of
nature which not only live but are intelligent
like myself.

But such beings belong, as I do myself, to
the external world of nature. It is in living
organisms that they express themselves for
me. Such organisms are, indeed, finite, and
conditioned by their senses. And yet I
accept them as in themselves standing for
subject in knowledge, just as I myself do.
They vary in the degree in which they express
mental qualities. All men are not alike.
Still less do even the higher animals stand
for mind as I find it in myself and in the

human beings I encounter. But at least in
the higher animals I seem to myself to
perceive what is distinctively of the nature
of mind. The elephant, the horse, and the
dog all understand up to a point. They
exercise free will and free choice, guided by
their understandings. They know nothing
of philosophy, but they know much of simpler
subjects belonging to their social life.

The presence in them, as well as in men, of
intelligence appears to be limited by brain
power. It is by this that their capacity for
general knowledge is determined. Some of
the higher animals have more and others have
less of this power. It is conditioned by
nervous organisation, and the various animals
can be classified into grades depending on
the quality of this. They do not reach
the standard of human beings, but not the
less they are up to a certain level intelligent, and have places in the world as
minds of their own quality.

The organisms which we perceive as included in the object-world are thus perceived
as minds. What we observe is conscious
and intelligent action of varying grades.
But the object is in such cases intelligence.
Mind finds itself in its object-world. That
world is not merely mechanistic, and is not
merely alive. It displays the qualities of

the self in a limited aspect, just as much as those of other forms of existence.

But the selves we become aware of are not all alike. A dog sees on the ground an insect. His instinct, which is partly racial, tells him that it is dangerous and may sting. It is a wasp, which he distinguishes from an adjacent bluebottle. Intelligent knowledge of a kind enters into the distinction. He sniffs it, keeping his nose at a distance. He touches it, but only with his claw. If he is sufficiently intelligent he may bite off its head and shoulders, spitting out the tail and the sting. The bluebottle he recognises as not dangerous and he eats it. He classifies in a rudimentary way which turns on possible sensations. It is his senses rather than general reasoning that he relies on. Still, he does appear to reason in a limited way in guiding his action. This we see him doing. We are observers of mind displaying itself in nature, mind in some degree resembling our own minds. The grade is different, but in both cases the object experience presents to us is one that knows, though the conceptions in which the external world is interpreted are neither so high as ours, nor so free nor of such range in the case of the dog.

The dog apparently finds his individuality

more confined than we do by his own living
organism. It is largely in sense experience
that he distinguishes himself from the world
in which he exists. He has no knowledge
of the grade required in order properly to
rationalise that world, so that difference
from himself may become, as with us, a
diminishing and even a disappearing one.
The negative limit of the particular hinders
largely in such knowledge as he has, and his
concepts and principles are comparatively
few. He does not find mind as the substance
of his object-world to the extent that we do.

For us also the physical situation of the
organism, and the limitations of the senses,
play a large part in distinguishing the not-
self from the self. But not so definite a part
For, as we have seen, in human experience
thought is recognised as entering into and
moulding the object. What we have as our
object in our consciousness of self is a self that
is indeed an object in the world, but an
object at a higher grade than that of any
other animal. It is an object which is
expressive of intelligence of a comparatively
high order. Still it not the less presents
itself in knowledge as an object in nature.
But nature and mind cease thereby to be
finally disseverable. The higher the grade
and range of intelligence the more does

there tend to disappear the exclusion of each by the other. That is what is meant when it is said that mind *finds* itself in nature.

Not the less the self in its ideal form, at the range which is only imperfectly attained in the human being whose mental powers are conditioned by the organism, is a self *for* which the world is there, a world which only by abstraction is dissevered from it. The power of reflection, in which general conceptions are dominant more than images, enables us to grasp the higher aspect of the human self, which extends the range of the knowledge which is of its essence limitlessly over the universe. Perfect and unhampered insight of this kind belongs to a level in knowledge which is not indeed foreign to our own, but is, as experience demonstrates, beyond its capacity to realise fully. Not the less idealistic reflection and the structure of experience itself both point towards an entirety of knowledge in which subject and object are no more than aspects falling within it.

But with the principle that the actual is experience it is vital from our standpoint to be in earnest. Too often this principle has had rendered to it mere lip service. It is stated, only to be almost immediately forgotten. Outside the direct and individual awareness which we find in self-consciousness we cannot get. We can analyse it through reflection so as to bring before thought the universals and ideals which fashion its expression, but the expression itself is not transcended in our immediate awareness. What is true of ourselves is true of all human beings. Others may excel us in their sense of the significance of symbols or in creative imagination. They may fall below us in these things as we think that the savage does. But the object-world appears as a common one for us all, however its appearances may vary in detail. For it is conditioned by the level above which the human organism is not capable of rising. The dog, with his flat head and limited brain, has a world which is in the main identical with ours, but he is precluded by his station in nature from fashioning it at the degree and with the range that are ours.

Still, in both cases what is foundational is knowledge, present indeed at different degrees. Such knowledge does not in the case of finite selves create its object-world; it only, by interpreting what it cannot control, fashions its existence. The world is an individual world and the interpretation takes place in conceptions that are general. That is the nature of our experience. It is the fact from which we start and behind which we cannot go. Only for mind different from ours could it be otherwise. For our experience is conditioned by the mind *for* which it is the actual.

But just as knowledge has degrees so the actual world has degrees which are manifested in the forms of its reality. It is there as a final fact, as the starting-point. But experience is no static abstraction. It is dependent for its very existence on reflection, and, as reflection is activity so is its creature activity. The sciences are the various modes in which it is resolved into general principles, no one of them ever exhaustive of all its aspects. The beautiful, the good, and the divine are aspects which experience presents for knowledge of kinds other than those which are appropriate to the special sciences for which they are required. The former illustrate values in experience, values which impose on us authority because of the constitution of our human minds, as do analogously the so-called laws of nature. All these belong to and enter into the very constitution of that experience which, as our object, is a final fact for our minds. But that experience, not being static and being interpreted with a boundless variety in the range of abstract reflection, is no foreign object that hems in the activity of the mind. It is only that which the mind has to accept and on which thought works.

Experience is no substance which can be dissected into parts, some of which are mechanistic, some biological, and some mental. It is dynamic activity that is constant in its exhibition of degrees and levels of varying kinds, all of which may characterise an object that remains identical throughout change in its various aspects. It is the content of our minds, including all that we see, feel, hear, taste, smell, and think about. All its phases are present in it, actually or imaginatively. They are aspects in an indivisible entirety, and it is only by abstraction that we isolate and sever them. That seems to be the character of the real as we are aware of it in our experience, not as separate from us but as there for the mind. That is what some of the greatest philosophers and observers that have lived have taken it to be and to signify. That is what Goethe in particular seems to have interpreted it as meaning for himself. No doubt it requires reflection to disentangle for us such meaning, and to enshrine it in general conceptions, and in our poetry and religion. But conceptions appear to be fundamental in knowledge and in reality. Our minds are not all alike, but in foundational character they not only resemble but are identical in the sense in which it is thought alone that, being no event in the external world, presents identity. It is to human nature that we have to turn for our starting-point, and it is to human nature, with the range that it has from being of the character of knowledge, that we come back. All science is simply the analysis of a content which is divisible only for reflection, and every doctrine of values is concerned with the same content. That this content can present itself at higher levels for knowledge the mind even of man tells us. But inconsistency and incongruity there is none.

We have now said enough of the relation between experience and actuality to enable us to proceed.

The work of reflection in the constitution of physical theory is a principle as much of the theory of knowledge as of mathematics. As long ago as 1893 the late F. H. Bradley, writing, not as a mathematician but as an exponent of the theory of knowledge, explained this and laid it down in its substance in his book on *Appearance and Reality*. He held as the result that there might be in our world a variety of wholly divergent systems of time and space, respectively relative to the observer. That was before Minkowski and Einstein had arrived at a similar result by mathematical methods. They were all three at one in holding that reflection has entered into the fundamentals of what had been too easily taken to be direct awareness unmoulded by thought, and, as reflection operates relatively, the circumstance might, they held, give rise to vastly important differences. That is the principle of the modern doctrine of relativity. It gets rid of undiscovered assumptions which were unconsciously moulding our view of what we seemed to know without apparent mediation from our thinking.

The entirety for presentation and reflection in which the object-world appears to become actual is thus a whole containing levels or degrees in which relations that are higher than we suppose may become obvious as we progress. The ideas of the inorganic and of life are not the only ideas required if reality is to be interpreted as it discloses itself in its fulness to be. For it is in knowledge and through it that meaning and existence are established and extended, and to the range of mind and of its work we do not know the limit. The ethical system of human society is not there for a rabbit, though for us it is actual. Nor have beauty or religion any significance for the rabbit. They simply do not exist. It is only for a mind at our own level that the world we know can be. Intelligent animals, like the ape or the elephant, may have experience of a world more nearly like our world, but our full world they do not experience. Outside possible experience there thus appears to be nothing actual. It is in its levels that the distinction between kinds of experience lies. Truth, beauty, goodness, these are facts of no world short of ours. They take us beyond order in externality, causation, living structure, into orders of a higher significance that are actual only for intelligence that is adequate to them and apart from which they are not. A dog is intelligent. He can separate out and guide sheep. He may understand directions given to him as to the chase of a wounded partridge in a turnip field. He may show delight in the flashing by of the objects he passes in the motorcar in which he is seated. But he will be unable to take in knowledge of a higher order. For his head is flat and indicates a limited development of his brain. It is the absence of higher brain organisation that limits the development of his mind. The organisation is no sufficient instrument for fuller intelligence. Just so insufficient brain power limits the scope of mind in the human beings of our object-world. An angel, if there be one, may have knowledge of a different degree, at which the particular, as a limiting factor, has diminishing significance. For particularity is, as we have seen, just a negative to the progress of thought, and we must not assume that such a negative has at every level of knowledge a function that is final, even in perception. In mind, as it confronts us in our object-world, restrictions appear to be bound up with physical form.

CHAPTER VII

THE SELF IN EXPERIENCE

IF the result of the inquiry up to this point be a true result, the relation of knowledge to the universe is a wholly different one from that set forth in Professor Dewey's book. Knowledge becomes for us the basis of that universe in a new sense. Knowing and being cannot in ultimate analysis be separable. To be present to mind as its object, actual or possible, past or present, is to *be* in the only meaning that ultimately attaches to existence. Within an entirety of which we cannot make a picture but towards which our reflection is compelled, subject and object fall as distinguishable only as phases within it.

Knowledge is thus foundational, and all that is, however apparently self-subsistent, is resoluble into forms of knowledge which extend to feeling and volition. This of course implies a revision of the idea of it as a property of some thing. There is nothing excepting as a phase in our object-world. In our experience we find the self that knows to be limited. That is because we find it

with a station in nature, as an object that is
conditioned in its selfhood. But even the
self so found implies a range beyond, a
range at which, at a higher level than that
of our finite minds, the unending pursuit
in experience of the particular culminates
in a conception of mind in which to think
must signify not less than to create. It
is to mind conceived as at this higher
degree that we seem driven for the solution
of a problem which concerns intimately the
character of experience as it discloses itself
to us, a problem which is apparently in-
soluble in any other way.

Mind itself presents aspects in which we
find it as belonging to our object-world. Only
under some such aspect are we conscious of
it as an individual object. Our consciousness
of self is of what is self included in our object-
world. I sit in a chair reflecting. It is
" I " who am reflecting, but an " I " who
am known to myself as a living organism,
seated in a particular chair. I may have
a further significance in the universe, but at
least I have this place. Without my living
brain I cannot think, nor can I apprehend
in perception excepting so far as I do so by
my organs of sense. These do not appear
to be instruments of any independently
existing entity called my soul. I have no

experience of any such independent object.
But my brain and organs are expressions
not only of what is alive but at a different
level of what thinks and feels. They are
themselves my soul in so far as they think
and feel, and as the instruments in which
thinking and feeling have to express themselves they limit my soul. Soul and body
are apparently not distinct or self-subsistent
entities. They seem rather to be the same
fact in different aspects, made what they
are under different sets of conceptions. The
operation of these different aspects is apparently involved in the signification of experience. They belong to different orders
in knowledge. But what at first glance
we take to be, in virtue of notions which
we have brought to bear, sensations directly
apprehended without mediation by reflection,
turn out when reflected on to signify sets
of general conceptions mediated by new
ideas as they progressively present themselves
in higher orders of knowledge. I see the
portion of the park lying before my window,
though I cannot see the more distant regions
of the city in which I live. Yet I have an
indirect or mediated experience of these
last. I have visited and remember the
more distant parts, and I know that they
exist and what they would be like if I went

there. I have seen them in the past, and I am convinced by reflection in general forms that if I went to them again I should have a similar experience. It is only through conceptions, which are general and being such can be defined, that they are now present to me. Even at this moment I form such conceptions of them by interpreting indications that come apparently directly to my senses from a distance. As regards the park at which I am now looking, what I have before me also implies the employment of further general notions, of life and of a society of human beings and of animals and plants. These are present in virtue of my faculty of interpretation, a faculty which a rabbit would not fully possess even if it should see as I do. It may show some interpretative capacity, but none at the higher levels of mine. The higher aspects do not in any intelligible sense exist for it, although they exist for a human mind.

We have experience, but what do we mean when we refer to the individual selves that have it ? The answer is we mean something of which we have experience. We mean organisms that know and have stations in nature from which they know. The self turns out to be more than a merely biological fact. It is an intelligent organism, and its

intelligence is of a human order. Inasmuch
as it is intelligent and knows it is no mere
thing. It is thus a centre and focus for its
experience, and is real just in that experience.
When it feels it does more than feel. It
interprets in conceptions. In such conceptions we never reach a final limit. Reflection
extends the range without assignable limit.
That is because reflection means thinking.
But the thinking that extends the range
and finds its nature in the process, although
limitless in its capacity, shows as it proceeds
more and more of general character the
further it reaches. We think no doubt in
images, but the images lose in definiteness
and detail the more we throw them in our
interpretations into system. The further we
progress, too, towards the conception of a
self that is to be all-inclusive of its world,
the more evasive does its individuality become. So far as our experience of this is
concerned we are driven, as in mathematics
and physics, to rely on investiture by reflection of such facts as we are concerned with.
And so in truth are we impelled in music
and in religion. These, too, have meaning
and existence only for the mind that can
reflect. It is only for the mind which thinks
that imagery has significance or reality.

The self thus turns out to be the central

activity in our thinking to which we refer
our experience and in which that experience
is centred.   It is not capable of being detached from and made in isolation from its
world an object for direct apprehension.
Itself the condition of experience it cannot
as such be an image to be discovered in it.
Not the less the perceptions which have their
unity in it imply the self as the source of the
active ideas which give them their significance.   It is in each of us foundational
of our experience, although in perception it
is not detachable from that experience.   It
is the activity in comprehension, identical
in all of us, which renders apprehension
actual as well as intelligible.   That was what
Kant told us long ago.   Only through the
resolutive power of mind, exercisable by
abstraction in concepts and not in any
concrete images, can we determine general
character in mind.   And yet it has no
objective existence separate from the experience into which it has entered.   The self
is always an individual self, although it is
and signifies more than this, and is not
detachable from its experience.   It is a self
which, because it expresses itself in an
organism, has a station in the object-world
of nature, and a name and identity there.
We cannot derive light on what this con-

clusion implies from analogies which are drawn from the outside world, nor yet from such a mathematical analogy as the centre of a circle. For such conceptions are mainly concerned only with order in externality. But the relation of the self in experience to its own experience is no relation of externality. Its experience is the self and the self is its experience. The relation is the final one of mind and an object which falls within mind. It is a relation in knowledge, brought to light by an act of abstraction which is in its essence conceptual. The mind and the object are no separate existences. They are aspects within an entirety the nature of which is to be all-inclusive.

From experience we set out, and apart from it, in actual or possible form, reality has no meaning. But experience is for the self no external object. The work of reflection, the activity of thought, is always present in it. The work of reflection can be apprehended only conceptually with reference to the subject in knowledge, but it is none the less implied in the object. The other side of this truth is that reflection gives us all we know of the self which, just like these, is incapable of being dissevered from the object-world.

Object and subject are thus not different

or distinct entities. On the contrary, each enters into the very nature of the other. It is only by abstraction, that is by excluding from reflection what is implied but yet does not concern our immediate purposes, that we speak of them as self-subsistent. Such abstraction is required for the advancement of knowledge and for facilitating definiteness in provisional definition, but it prevents us from being aware of the whole of our subject-matter. Just because our knowledge requires its methods we are confronted with the necessity of abstraction at every turn of thought. In order to be complete knowledge must therefore be explained as including not only its object but the character of its own processes. All that is, was, and can be, falls within it, and it is thus foundational to reality. But if this be so, and if knowledge exhibits levels in the notions applied in it, and degrees depending on these levels, then the levels and degrees which knowledge exhibits must display themselves also in the universe which is the object of knowledge. Art and religion, in so far as they are concerned with our actual experience, will have their significance in their own ideas, ideas which may be, both in fact and in logic, irreducible to those of science without conflicting with the principles which rule there. For the two sets of ideas belong to different domains of knowledge, and the principles on which they base themselves belong in the case of each set to its own domain in knowledge and reality. They have logically distinct places in the full system of knowledge, taken in its largest sense, and in experience they do not conflict, when we bear in mind that the domains to which they belong are domains of wholly distinct orders, which must never be confused or sought to be reduced to each other.

The individuality that is characteristic in art redeems at once the formlessness of mere feeling, and the emptiness of mere generality divorced from its bodily expression, by the determining power of reflection. In the object of art the two aspects which enter into the real ought to be indissolubly united by the artist's faculty of imagining individual forms. His gift is required to lift the picture or the poem above the transience of common-place experience, and to fill with significance of a high kind what by itself can be at most a bare symbol. It is in meaning here again that the truth lies for the artist. The meaning cannot be rendered in the ordinary universals of inference. It is expressed pictorially and depends on the sensuous quality of the image created, as well as on a level in interpretation. The universal comes in, but does not present itself as abstract in the art that is of the highest kind. It comes in only in a concrete symbol into which the work of thought enters, but not into anything that can exist without the co-operation of sensuous imagination.

What is actual in art is therefore of a nature that in itself has a varying material. But it is what it is because of that aspect in it that remains changeless, and is not dependent on the time and space to which belongs the element of feeling. The object of art is thus what abides through change, and this is true of painting, of poetry, of music, of every form of art. It is also true of the religious consciousness. It is the revelation of what is not subject to time or space in those to whom it has come that gives to them the sense that in this kind of knowledge the ordinary problems of life are not only transcended but have ceased to present themselves. So far as it can in the ordinary sense be called knowledge, such knowledge is of a different level from that of science. The relations of order in externality which have become for most purposes the beginnings of wisdom, have ceased to be the end of wisdom.

It is thus that art and religion lift us

above what is merely transient and contingent, however much their metaphors and similes may be drawn from the passing experiences of daily life.

Let it not be supposed that this view of the actual as fashioned by mind in knowledge of different orders affects the principles and procedure on which science rests. In physical science, for example, we are concerned with relations and aspects of things that are inseparable from order in externality and from certain other orders in our experience. None of these hinder or are hindered by the work of reflection in isolating the aspects which belong to the domain of science. There is no conflict simply because the conceptions under which science makes and can only make its abstractions are of a nature different from those implied in art and religion. If we keep the orders to which the different kinds of conception belong distinct in our consideration of them we see why they do not conflict. A sunset means one thing for the artist and quite a different thing for the physicist, who is not for the moment concerned with beauty or with imaginative investiture. It is only when in either case we set up rigid metaphors and affirm them to be exhaustive descriptions of the real that conflict arises. If we remember

that in neither case is the description more
than symbolic of a reality so full that it has
many aspects, and that the symbols employed
have been determined by conceptions sever-
ally indicated to us by our special experiences,
but logically so different that they do not
conflict, we shall be delivered from per-
plexities that are present only because we
have created them by our exclusive views.
It will remain as true as before that the
physicist must proceed by methods which
are strictly those once inspired by his inheritance from men like Bacon, and are
founded on observation and experiment. All
he is asked to do is to keep in mind that
by such methods he can no more exhaust
the many-sided aspects which experience
presents than his comrade the mathematician can exhaust them by the methods of
algebra.

But the other extreme has equally to be
avoided. Art and religion speak directly
because they speak in metaphors and similes.
But these, although they imply conceptions
which belong to their own orders, aspects
which are necessary if the truth about
reality is to be fully given, do not express
what is alone true from the standpoint of
science. Into the domain of science they
have no title to intrude or to question what

its special principles establish. The levels are different as regards both knowledge and the reality to which it is directed. The conceptions employed are of necessity of different orders. That is why art and religion on the one hand and science on the other do not conflict, if we only interpret and limit their deliverances aright.

CHAPTER VIII

HOW MEANING ENTERS INTO REALITY

PEOPLE are perplexed when they are told
that it is meaning that gives its reality to
the actual. They imagine that the actual
is what is there independently of the thoughts
of the spectator. Now that is from the
point of view of the daily practice of men
quite true, and it would be so from a standpoint more searching if the object observed
could be taken to be in truth one thing and
the mind that observes it another. But is
this " two substance " view a tenable one ?
It assumes knowledge to be a property or
activity of a thing called the mind. No doubt
we do at many standpoints and for ordinary
purposes treat the object we observe as
completely self-subsistent, shutting out from
it all intrusion of ideas. We image to ourselves the mind as a thing located somehow
in the brain, and passively looking out on
its object as another thing with which the
mind coexists in the world. But is this
enough ? It will be insufficient if the interpretation that has in the end to be put on
our knowledge and the meanings in which

it results is, not that knowledge is an event apart from the existence of the object, but that it is the activity of thought entering into the constitution of the object itself. If so, by the mind we have properly intended to speak of knowledge itself in the largest sense, and of it as more than any mere happening to the individual organism. If to know implies what is no merely passive reception of isolated sensations, but signifies that these sensations are present for us only in so far as they are set in knowledge itself as a system, then reality apart from knowledge seems to vanish. Now we can bring this to the test. For if we find that in order to make it possible for what is observed to be a fact for all men who observe it they must observe under the same conditions, which can only be the case if they interpret it through conceptions which are theirs in common and identically, this will go far to show that it is in the identity of logical conceptions applied, in other words in identity of interpretation, that the reality of a common object-world consists.

Our best way of making a test appears to be to start from some concrete and individual experience, and to disentangle its significance. It is so that we can most easily see the distinction implied between

notions of universal application such as
we find in our experience, and the particulars of sensation which they seem to
qualify.

Let us imagine that we are in a crowd that
is listening to an orator in a park. It consists, we will suppose, of two hundred English-
men, all with ears with which they hear and
with eyes with which they see. We put
things only elliptically when we say that
the orator addresses them. What he actually
does is to move his hands and his features
and to fashion with his lips waves in the air
which come as sounds to the listeners. Their
visual perception of his gestures, on the other
hand, is not less indirect, for it is based on
electro-magnetic waves in what is sometimes
called the ether.

The waves of air fall on the drums of the
listeners' ears, and the waves of light produce
chemical changes in the retinas of their
eyes and so stimulate the optic nerves.
There thus arise in the individual members
of the audience sensations or feelings of these
two kinds. They affect the individual organisms privately. They are events in the
inner life of each individual in which no
others can participate directly. The domain
of each private self is impenetrable and can
be recognised only by description in terms

which are altogether general. Such terms
are names for interpretations through conceptions, fashioned by logical processes in
which feelings are classified and in that way
identified. But the feelings themselves
are beyond the reach of direct description.
There is in them a formless particularism
which can never be exhausted. All that is
possible is to describe the similarity of someone's feeling to the feeling of another person,
and such similarity, depending as it does
on a common understanding of the language
heard and the gestures seen, is necessarily
of a merely general or conceptual nature,
signifying that each man in the audience
attaches a similar meaning to the words and
events, and so employs similar ideas in con-
struing the feelings which are particular
happenings pertaining to him alone. The
common bond is the conceptual identity which
presents itself right through an infinity of
minute differences. It is in other words only
for reflection, that is for mind, that the same
object exists and is recognised as the same.
The identity of the common world observed
lies in sameness to a sufficient extent in
what is a common intellectual process of
recognition.

The element of sensation in the general
experience is essential, for without it there

would be mere general reflection determining nothing actual. In all human experience the factor of the particular comes in as well as that of the universal of thought. But neither can reach reality apart from the other. The individuality that characterises actual experience embraces both as factors or moments which are essential for its constitution. Deprived of either of these the individual experience could not be actual, and each of them is only actual as entering into individual knowledge so constituted. But when we know and formulate and express our knowledge it is on the universal element alone that we have to concentrate ourselves. That of the bare particular eludes us. We cannot fasten on it in its own isolated nature because it has no nature that we can describe to ourselves in any terms. It is a residuary factor which we cannot exhaust or even reach or define, a limit towards which we proceed as we endeavour to cover the whole character of the individual object of our experience by description in general terms. But it is a limit to which we approach only asymptotically, that is to say, we never can come up to it. If we could, then our mere ordinary reflection would create actual experience, and this for us it never does.

Let us now turn to the other aspect of experience and ask in what knowledge consists. In knowledge we so far find true identity. Logical conceptions can be identical just as much as logically they can be different. For they are not happenings or events in an external world of space and time, occurrences which can only be compared as separate objects of perception, and pronounced to be like or unlike to each other. They belong to the activity of thought for which space and time as relations of objects to the observer are there, but as thoughts about objects they are not themselves events external to the mind that determines them. They can therefore be identical in the strictest sense. A proposition of Euclid, though printed on my paper and not on his papyrus, is in logic an identical proposition for me and for him. Mind in its proper sense here means simply the activity of thought which as it determines our logic is thus identical in us. Of course psychologists by abstraction, and by what is always a distortion of their final character, often treat the activities of thought as though they were objects which could be looked at as if external to the observer. The Behaviourists carry this to its full consequences. We are conscious that we are minds within a world, and in this

sense we are aware of activities in reflection
that are bodily as well as mental. But our
knowledge and the object are in this case
treated as indistinguishable, and the procedure of the psychologist, in concentrating
on certain aspects exclusively of others, is
artificial. We are aware that knowledge
changes and we are conscious also of the
nature of the changes. It is now six o'clock.
Presently it will be five minutes past six.
When the sequence of impending events is
accomplished, what is "now" will have
become "then." But "now-ness" and
"then-ness" are not events which happen
and which we hold out, as it were, at arm's
length and observe. They are in the nature
of relations in our perception of the world,
adjectival to ourselves, and different for
observers under different conditions, as the
modern doctrine of physical relativity tells
us. They are, in short, modes in which
mind exercises its activity in thought, references to itself which it makes in reflection,
and not qualities of objects by our abstraction regarded as independent of us. It is
as such modes of its own procedure that
reflection is aware of them and recognises
them as adjectives of an application which
is wholly general in character, even when
applied to the particular circumstances of

the object-world. They are, in brief, no more than universals of reflection.

Such considerations carry us yet further. The view that seems to account best for the actual facts of experience is that by the conceptions in which reflection progresses we do not simply form the vague and loose images which mere words are usually taken to indicate. We do not really in reflection disregard the particularities which appear to confront us. We rather seek to show just the necessity of the occurrence and relations of these particularities. It is not the " universality " of an isolated presentation that we aim at, but the universal validity of a system and a principle of order. The concrete universality so attained belongs to the systematic whole, which takes up into itself the particularities falling within it, and develops them into a systematic entirety according to a principle. The function of reflection, and of all induction, is therefore to be actively transformative, and not merely to be receptive. The procedure is not from inert things and their common properties, but from relations between concepts reached in the progressive rendering of reality in knowledge. We do not copy ; we are not static ; we pass from pictorial to functional expressions.

For instance, the conception of the physical

" field " in Faraday's sense is a new mediating and functional conception, bringing together what we call " matter" and " empty space." Thereby modern physics gains, and not least from an epistemological point of view, a sharper and more distinct idea of its subject-matter. Faraday reconstructed the conception of matter by treating it as arising out of " lines of force." What he arrived at was that the field made up of force does not depend on matter, but that matter is nothing but specially distinguished phases in the lines in this field. The doctrine has been since his time much further elaborated by means of the equations of electrodynamics. Such developments, arising in various branches of science, are having a far-reaching effect on the theory of induction, now based on the recognition of relations, only to be expressed conceptually, that enter genuinely into the constitution of the individual objects of experience. A great deal of work is being done in the subject on the Continent by men of science themselves.[1]

Let us now return to the consideration of the experience of the crowd.

[1] See, for example, Professor Ernst Cassirer's remarkable account of this work in his *Substanzbegriff und Functionsbegriff* (English Translation by Swabey).

Each of the two hundred listeners to the orator has his own sensations of sight and sound, and, as we have seen, these sensations are comparable only in the meanings arising from their setting in reflection, and not as bare self-subsisting and exclusively private sensations. The listeners are certain that they see and hear the same man. Their bare sensations cannot tell them this, for these are transitory and formless and are not, taken by themselves, of any significance at all. It is surely in the common meaning which all incorporate with their feelings that perception of the actual lies. More than this, the common meaning and the reality of its occasion are not distinguishable when we analyse them. The feeling and its interpretation are not and cannot be dissociated in what is actual. Neither is real excepting as entering into the other. The mere sensation could not be known, the mere reflection would be less even than a vague impression, or an unreal image, such as is a dream. Mind in the listener requires reference to the position and state of his organism for its expression in him. The identity in the experiences of the two hundred has to be sought for in the common references made in these experiences by those who have them, that is to say, in their common mode of reflection. That explains, too, why they can communicate them to each other. What is the nature of such communication ? The members of the audience reflect in forms or modes which are relatively identical from the standpoint of logic. But there might be a different level, as in the case of a beetle among the feet of the crowd, or of a dog who had intruded to seek for food, or who hoped at least for some attention from those listening to the speech, or even in that of the foreigner who could see gestures that seemed to indicate patriotism or religious emotion, but could not make out the words used. The process of perception by the crowd is a conceptual one, although its concepts embrace within their general character many individual possibilities. Such concepts are therefore general, and are meaningless if we try to treat them as merely particular events in the space and time of the object-world. They belong to thinking. If we were to say that universals like these were themselves facts felt in the object-world we should find ourselves in the difficulty that all such facts would be individual in character, that is to say, they must embrace the moment of the particular in order to exist as facts that are actual. In such a case it could only be by disentangling the moment of the universal in them that we could know them, and we should be thrown back towards another line of reasoning which finds nothing but universals in our perception. To be a man is to come within a class, a conception of general application. To be an orator is still to belong to a class, a sub-class of that of man. In such instances it is with predicates of a universal character that we are concerned when we perceive and in perceiving judge. Now what the audience does in the case we are considering is to make in common various interpretations of the speaker. Quite consistently with their common interpretations he may appear differently to those in the audience individually. Some of them may be short-sighted, or colour-blind, or unusually ignorant. But in the essentials required for a common experience relevant to the purpose in hand they all judge him in much the same way. This they do because they think identically in concepts appropriate to the purpose in hand, which is to hear and estimate the speaker. The beetle or the dog that had strayed into the crowd would judge differently. Their standards would not be the same. Their notions, so far as they had any, and their mental levels would be lower, and their concepts would fall short of what was required to make their interpretations equal to those of the human beings. We should not find in them that identity in conceptual understanding that was requisite in order to constitute the experience of a meeting for a public purpose. For them the State does not exist. But for men it does, inasmuch as they bring identical knowledge at a sufficient level into the interpretation of significance. That is how the experience of the meeting has come to be actual. Meaning is not only of the essence of that actuality, but the interpretation out of which it arises enters into its constitution, and all experience is relative to it.

The factor of sensation in such constitution of the actual is dependent on the organism of the observer. If the organism does not have sensations the experience, however lucid, is not a real one enjoyed in common. That is why a dream picture, however unlimited and vivid it may be in our version of it, although in itself a fact for the dreamer, is never a reality for other people. The element of continuity of the body with the surroundings pictured is absent, as we find when we awaken and bring our ideas to the test of harmony with the full context of these surroundings, and of the lives of our neighbours. In order to participate in what is actual for others as well as for ourselves we must recognise it as possible for their organisms as well as for our own, a possibility which depends not only on universals but on sensations which are invested with the character of generality in our recognition of them. Such recognition is in point of fact inferential. When I say that if I walk farther I shall come to the next street, that is not because I perceive directly, but because I infer from my present experience as interpreted another and a different experience which I forecast from a general interpretation of existing experience. My knowledge is based on the system into which reflection has cast my usual experience, and into this system I expect reality to fit. But much more than bare sensation is required to explain the origin of the system of such experience.

Now the experience of those at the meeting is just of this nature. Their sensations of sight and hearing are all individual, but the interpretation, arising as it does from the character of the subject in knowledge which is no thing, is in all essentials identical and unavoidable. This does not signify that the sensations exist independently and afford by themselves some sort of limited reality. Nor does it import that the concepts of the onlookers are applied to them arbitrarily. For abstract universals cannot constitute the actual any more than bare sensations can. The two are actual only in their union in the individual and unique fact actually experienced. This fact implies both in its constitution, and it is only within the fact thus constituted that the general and the particular, the concept and the feeling, are recognised and logically distinguished as separable. We saw how the resolution thus made into universals by reflection is for mind operating in the orders with which we are familiar an unending one, confronted by the particularism of feeling as a negation or limit which is never reached nor fixed in independence. Whenever we seem to have fixed it as an independent fact we find that we have only done so by bringing to light fresh universals of reflection. But in the actual facts of experience from which we start both moments are implicit in their union. We shall have to ask how it is that the mind which seems to be identified with a particular organism can be taken to be so important a factor in the constitution of the reality which we pronounce to be independent of it, and we shall find that our difficulty arises from our taking too narrow a view of the nature of the mind. We shall see that it *finds* in the object with which it is one both universal and particular, and does not, in the metaphorically imaged and narrow way in which we have conceived it, create them. But not the less it finds by its process of abstraction through reflection universals which are of its own character and are like itself activities of mind without which the object could have no meaning and could not be. This we shall have to consider further later in the inquiry.

Meantime, what seems to result so far as we have gone is that the actual meeting, the speaker and his speech and his audience, require for their full realisation as facts a certain level of intelligence. A foreigner who did not understand the language would recognise that there was a crowd and someone talking to it. He would thus know much more than the beetle or the dog. But he would not know what the occasion signified for the others present, or what they were saying to each other or thinking among themselves. For the members of the audience, when they interchanged ideas about the subject of the speech, could only do so in words or gestures which again came under general conceptions that were familiar to them only because their minds were sufficiently furnished.

We seem unable to get away from the conclusion that the minds of the listeners are minds only in virtue of some sort of identity in their activity and method of judgment and interpretation. But if so, mind can hardly be just a mode in which these listeners have sensations. In what the character of mind lies is a question to which we must give further attention.

CHAPTER IX

INDIVIDUALITY IN EXPERIENCE

WHAT is real for us is thus our experience. Its form is individual. Universals therefore enter into its constitution and accordingly reflection presents it to our minds in general conceptions. But our world of experience is nothing that can be, as it were, held out at arm's length, and broken up into any aggregate of fragments. The physicist seems sometimes to assume that it can be, but that is obviously because his method is that of abstraction. He shuts out the relation of his object to mind, and from the dynamic activity of mind he severs the experience with which he is dealing. That is not a wrong method. It is the only one that can serve his purpose, which is to exhibit special principles in his subject-matter, principles of the kind required for simplification and definiteness. His method is that of all effective human knowledge and he is fully within his rights in using it. But he must not forget that he has shut himself off by using it from any full vision of the actual, and that he is resolving this into sets

of abstractions. Now our world is no set
of abstractions, nor is our knowledge of it
all of one kind.

Experience has levels in its individual
forms, and what is actual for us accordingly
also displays such levels. It is the recognition of this that delivers us from difficulties
in accepting what experience teaches. It is
clear that experience is no fixed or static
entity. It is rather a dynamic process which
inherently depends on reflection, and is
self-evolving and self-explicating in its integrity. Always individual of its kind, it
drives us to seek for particularism as such
as well as for the aspects of generality which
are characteristic of reflection. In experience
the mind is constantly varying the setting
in which the object is presented to the
intelligence that construes it. It is in what
are the identities in thinking which this
process of investing brings to light that
what we call objective reality seems to lie.
It is identity of this kind that we mean when
we speak of the object as the same even
through different aspects of knowledge about
it. My neighbour has his distinctive chemical structure and is yet the identical social
figure that I know. For this structure is
only one out of his many aspects and does
not explain the activities of his mind. Yet

there is no object that is actual for the human mind or even intelligible to it apart from that moment of the particular the nature of which we have already discussed. This particularity in experience human reflection does not exhaust and it does not create it. It is essential in what is actual, but its nature is of a merely negative or limiting kind, and yet is such that our reflection cannot construct or even describe it. Not the less is it implied in the constitution of all human experience.

For the significance of the activity that is characteristic of our knowledge we must look below a surface that is strewn with our own abstractions. Knowledge is not constructed or put together mechanically, by adding conceptions and particulars to each other. An individual form in which these are not dissevered appears to be the real form in which knowledge discloses itself in self-consciousness. Such knowledge is not static, and it is by abstract methods of self-development that never take account of all that is implied, that disseverance in our reflection comes about. The process is never adequate to the full reality. In our experience mind and its object are there as one and indivisible. But the movement of experience is dynamic in the impulse to disentangle by reflection the universals that

enter into the constitution of what we feel
and see and smell and taste and hear and
touch. We do more than merely disentangle.
For we are conscious of experience as en-
larging, as the result of its very nature, its
own scope and its own actual standpoints.
The identities of which we become aware
in perception and conception alike imply
selves that know and are more than isolated
and static units. The human being, and
something of the same sort is true of the
conscious animal, is unintelligible as a merely
living organism. As a comprehending self
of some kind it finds itself in relation to a
society of other selves, and its relation to
these other selves is a foundational one of
identity amid divergences which it interprets.
Mind is no thing fixed once for all as an
event or activity in space and time. When
for purposes that are only partial we identify
it with the organism, even conceived as
intelligent, we have not understood all there
is to understand about it. We are in truth
here as elsewhere more than we have taken
ourselves to be. Minds are actually as well
as logically identical as they think identically
in conceptions. So far as the knowledge of
different persons is indistinguishable in its
content, it is to that extent no separable
set of activities, but is logically one and the

same, however separated may be in time
and space the physical persons who think.
Thinking can be no property of the organism.
It is the *prius* required in order that there
may be an object-world at all. The subject,
when we refer it back far enough, we find
to show the knowledge for which the object-
world *is*. It is activity, but it is the activity
of mind as such, and not merely of any
particular mind in its aspect as a particular
object. It is not through the senses but
only in concepts that we reach it, and yet,
because it is the centre to which we have to
refer the whole of our experience, it is in
that sense individual. But this individuality
is such that it seems to reach over all particular experience, although it requires such
experience for its self-realisation. Thus experience lifts itself, by the dialectical quality
which is inherent in knowledge, to new levels.

In art, the character of the universal
raises to a higher level what is in its primary
aspect of an everyday nature. The mother
of Christ and her Child are from the ordinary
human standpoint in the picture of them
like any other mother and child. Yet the
genius of a great artist changes the standpoint to a different one, at which we interpret
the picture before us through new and
higher ideas that enter in. The simplicity

of nature is there, but it yields to and is
made to symbolise what is more than mere
nature. When a great painter brings before
us a Highland burn he tells us of features
which we may see any day. But he invests
the scene with a quality that is symbolic
of something more. He expresses for us
no merely casual features of the landscape,
but by stimulating reflection suggests that
which transports us beyond what is mo-
mentary. We have in our minds a character interpreted as belonging to the universal
and eternal, to reflection and not only to
sense. So when we hear a sonata or a
nocturne we may be lifted above the music
of the moment to a frame of mind where
that music stands for something else than
what is simply pleasing to us, something
in which we realise that time and space are
not even for us final, but fall within ourselves.

To the mere animal none of these things
are open, even when he is intelligent. He
is deficient in the necessary concepts. Experience at the requisite level comes only to
mind that has at least a capacity such as
we human beings have. For such mind
alone is capable of entering into and absorb-
ing all possible meanings. There is experience
of this sort only for such a mind.

That, too, is why the mere animal has no

religion. For religion has significance and is a fact only for the mind that can lift itself to its level, and knows what it signifies to be ready to surrender the will and to die in order to live. Still, it must not be thought that the mind of an animal is incapable of higher levels than those that are its common levels. No one who has been in affectionate relations with a devoted dog can have failed to notice how his attitude to his master becomes one of regarding that master as a being of a superior order, to whom at times he accords something like reverence. There is here some analogy to nascent religion.

The function of education is not to create the higher attitudes of the soul, but only to render them more readily attainable. The good man may not be educated. The educated man may not be good. But education does render it easier for the mind to emancipate itself to higher levels. For it enables abstractions and partial views to be recognised by which the real has been crusted over and confined, and it thereby delivers the soul from fetters that have restrained its self-development.

But we must be clear as to the place in experience of what we call knowledge. As we find ourselves driven to give so important a place to knowledge we must consider what is its true nature. It seems to be distinguished in a material respect from that to which the word " experience " is commonly applied. When we use the latter term we make implied reference to the knowledge and feeling of particular persons. The particular person is in a prominent aspect an organism with a station in space and time. Not the less do we regard him as a subject that knows, but knows under the condition that he is himself an object in the world. If I ask what my self is I cannot get away from the idea that it sits in a chair, even when it is surveying the universe in its reflection. We must not make the assumption that because in one aspect it sits in a chair there is some numerically different self that is subject in knowledge. It is quite conceivable that mind may be object in nature as well as, at the same time but from another point of view, subject in reflection about nature. When we think of ourselves as merely having feelings these are always the feelings of a mind that is a body. But, here as elsewhere, when the object is set in reflection it is set in general conceptions, and the language in which we describe these is never directed to anything excepting general notions. In other words, it is never exhaustive of the actual. Although we take ourselves to be here and now, so do other people who are for us there and then. We all use concepts which apply equally, with the necessary modifications, to a plurality of individual instances. It is our standpoints that make the difference, and standpoint may depend on view as to position in space and time, as well as on view as to other circumstances.

In all such cases we are brought back to the universals in which we think identically as our common basis, and it is as referred to these universals that we use the word knowledge. The experience in which knowledge is expressed presupposes it as the condition of its possibility, but it actually describes what is of more limited application, knowledge as expressing itself under restricting conditions. None the less these conditions are themselves meaningless except as set in universals of reflection. The presupposition of capacity for such reflection is required in the perception even of the barest feeling. I cannot recognise my own sensations as occurring in a series unless I can hold them to some extent together, and this I can only do if I recognise a general character which I call their resemblance. The merest feeling has some general quality in which it resembles a different feeling. This seems to be the true explanation of the principle of the association of ideas. It is, moreover, only by comparison based on inference from their behaviour that I become aware that other people have feelings resembling my own, and that my mind so finds itself in them. Apart from recognition of an universal character in it feeling is meaningless and is no more there for me. Even bare awareness implies judgment, however rudimentary, through general conceptions.

It is thus that we appear to come by systematic knowledge. If we identify it with experience in which a self expresses its nature, we call it the experience of that self, notwithstanding that such experience is being progressively resolved into universals. The thoughts that are found in analysis to constitute it are always more than happenings in space and time, for they are without the particularism of these. We may regard them from a limited standpoint as events, but we have always to bear in mind that such a standpoint is in itself inadequate to the actual, inasmuch as it ignores the way in which thought enters in all contemplation. The psychologists when they use psychological methods are justified in doing so only to the same extent as the physiologist is justified when he works with the methods of physics and chemistry, but neither can realise in this fashion the whole truth. Mind and its object are never separable excepting by abstraction. When I perceive, my attitude and aspect are those of subject in knowledge, and I bring universals to bear. Could I reduce to terms what I perceive, by some searching method such as that called in the language of mathematical logic the method of extensive abstraction, I should be left in the end with general concepts as the outcome. These I should recognise as entering into the nature of the object of my study. For the object can never be divested of the work of thought as entering into the constitution of its reality.

To be subject is to be more than a mere isolated phenomenon in the object-world of experience. I am sitting in a room, writing at a table. The table is clearly no part of myself. Nor are my clothes, although they may be characteristic of my individuality in some measure for others as well as for myself. Nor is my little finger myself, for I could get on without it. Nor are any of my organs myself, nor indeed my body as a whole. No doubt I should die if these were destroyed, and I should not any longer be known by others as existing. I might also cease to signify " me " for myself. But implied for the possibility and presence in

my world of all these is the self that is more
than any of them. If they are gone it may
no longer exist in time or be aware of itself
as in any way expressed in them. But,
when they were there, they and the space
and time in which they were related to me,
the future, the present, and the past, implied
the self apart from which none of them had
any meaning. The activity of such a self
thus could not have been an event in the
space and time which required it as the condition of their own presence, but must have
been of another nature, that of knowledge
or mind, if we like to call it so, a condition
of events but not itself one among them.
Knowledge or mind is what holds the entirety and all its details together, including
relations in space and time. Apart from
their presence to knowledge these would
be meaningless and therefore unreal. Universals are vital to their actuality, and it
is only through universals that they have
any significance for ourselves or for others.

We must try to be more definite as to
what the subject signifies. So far we have
only distinguished it as what is essential
as a foundation in knowledge.

CHAPTER X

THE FOUNDATION OF THE ACTUAL

WE came very early to the conclusion that the nature of the real was to be found in our experience, that this experience was individual in character, and that therefore, being individual, reflection with its general conceptions entered into it. The real is inseparable from knowledge. But the work of knowledge always calls for explanation. It may be true that our knowledge does not create or even exhaust reality. That may well be the case, consistently with the fact that apart from subject, object is not possible. But the way of deliverance from obscurity seems to be to treat the two aspects, which reflection distinguishes, subject and object, as falling together in an entirety within which the universe comes, and to look on neither aspect as actual apart from its correlative in that entirety.

The subject cannot be as such a self-subsistent object for perception. For it is what is required to make it conceivable that there should be such an object at all, and is the condition of the object having any significance. Just because it is only for the subject that a world can have any meaning, and just because it is as having meaning that the things we know are in the end to be interpreted as real, we find the subject, treated abstractly as reflection treats it, and taken by itself, to be no more than what we may call a limiting conception in our experience, an ideal towards which the nature of that experience compels us to strive without our being able to present it in pictorial form. It is through the principle already referred to of degrees or levels that manifest their presence both in knowledge and in external reality that the object discloses to us its character as significant of an essential relation to the self.

In terms that are general and belong to reflection only we can express how it is that the subject does not wholly evade us. In self-consciousness we are aware of the activity of knowledge, not as if it were any object external to reflection, but as present in the object for reflection turned on itself, and aware of itself in that reflection. Such knowledge seems to disclose itself as self-consciousness in the thinking which is of its essence. The validity of knowledge in general we cannot question. For it is no external instrument with which the mind works, but really is just the mind itself as the activity in which our consciousness of the universe consists. This activity is one behind which we cannot go, simply because we can only try to do so by making use of and so relying on it. Knowledge cannot analyse itself into anything outside itself. For it is itself the foundation and the essence of every act of analysis. It is present to us not as a detachable aspect of the real but as our own mental activity, inseparable from the self and operating at levels or degrees that are divergent. We may doubt particular conclusions, but a completely sceptical view of knowledge is impossible, for it at once defeats itself. Knowledge as such is no means to anything beyond itself. It is no instrument, no way to truth beyond knowledge. Its criticism is self-criticism, the recognition in itself of that development which belongs to the inherent nature of mind in its freedom. This is the " I " to which we are always driven back. It is not as such an individual object in nature, for its character lies in universals the operation of which remains always general, although it transforms objectivity. The " I " is expressed in personality. Personality finds itself in an external world, hypostatising itself by abstraction from its own nature

in the idiosyncrasy of the individual organism
which, although it is intelligent as well as
living, has a place in time and space. But
even when personality assumes the form for
itself of a mere one among many, of a plurality
of selves, it still refers back to what is its
foundational form, the knowledge for which
its world is.

It is thus that the self prevents itself as
expressing its activity at levels which are
more than it takes itself in its immediate
object form to possess. Its organism knows
as well as feels. The form of a living object
that has experience implies in that experience both aspects. In it they are related
as belonging to different levels, but are not
disseverable. They indeed comprise aspects
under which mind presents to itself a world
which includes the self, unless we make
abstraction from what belongs to the character of mind alone. It is within the range
of reflection that the real is presented. It
can only be adequately so presented in that
under its higher aspects it falls within and
belongs to mind itself.

We come so to a deeper view of the self
than that of the psychologist. The real is
of course beyond our individual control, and
is independent of the self so far as this is
conceived, as the psychologist conceives it,

only in the form of a particular object in nature. But, although the individual self can be treated by abstraction as being this, it is in truth more. It is what in a more general aspect is identical in the strictest sense in all individual selves. It is their foundation apart from which they and their worlds would have neither meaning nor reality. The full self must be interpreted through conceptions at a degree higher than those which suffice for the observation of mere events. As reflection develops, the character of the conceptions to which it finds itself thus impelled becomes apparent. Freedom and creative activity are not ideas which we encounter as relations in time and space. Of levels higher than these, and of corresponding degrees in reality, there may be various orders. Our logic indeed discloses progressive variety in these orders, progressive in so far as the further we get the more do they prove adequate to the comprehension of what we are faced with in what reflection tells us of our fuller nature. We can obviously form no *picture* of objects belonging to any order that, because it is too high for pictorial form, is reached only in the universals of reflection. But the process of growing self-comprehension impels us towards an ideal. It is that of a self

beyond numerical distinction, and yet identical even as disclosed in numerically distinct
selves.   For such a self is no " event."   From
what we have already seen this is no strange
view if the real nature of mind is to be looked
for as akin to thought with its universals,
and not in any mere particularism of sense
which has its significance only when presented
in thought as an apparently independent
object.   The self in this higher meaning is
unlimited, as thought itself is unlimited.   It
stretches in reflection over its universe, as
our thoughts do—without barrier.   It is
what gives their character to the various
orders in experience, and founds progressively
different degrees in reality, such as include
causes, ends, and freedom.   In this aspect
the universe falls within mind, and we are
faced in it with the inner universe of which
Goethe spoke, a universe which takes up
into itself that which at first, in a view that
abstractly dissevers, appears to be independent of it.   For it is only for the self
as expressed in the forms and at the level
of nature, as a finite mind expressed in an
organism with a period and station there,
that sense perception is marked off from
knowledge, and that particular and universal
are split asunder as though they could be
objects of independent natures.   Here, within

the entirety, we become progressively cognisant of the severance as superseded, and
from the new standpoint we are forced so
to conceive it. The negation or limit which
is all that the particularism of sense consists
in becomes transcended.

At such a standpoint a fuller reflection
than that which is employed in everyday
social life teaches us to recognise the meaning
of the ideal for which we have to search.
Yet an ideal it remains. We cannot see or
hear it. We may indeed express in the
metaphors of art and religion the conceptions
it implies, but they are metaphors which are
drawn from sense experience and they are
no more than symbolic of what they really
signify. What they point us to has a character that may be called " absolute," because dependent on nothing at a lower level
than itself, the very foundation and nature
of the universe without and within. But
here as elsewhere when the word " absolute "
is employed it is employed as indicative of
a degree in knowledge rather than of a final
result attained. There is indeed no legitimate
meaning for final truth in this connection.
For us it seems rather to be in the continuous
and conscientious employment of a method
of reflection that can never be wholly freed
from the relativity of the everyday stand-

points to which we limit ourselves in the daily experience which is ours, that the highest truth for us consists.

Of God we can have no pictorial vision. But if we recognise that he is not conceivable excepting as immanent and as not less than in that way personal, we lose nothing. The symbols of art and religion enable us to have a vivid sense of his nature. We require their constant aid, even if we cannot ask them for a satisfying view of the foundations of the real. If we have that aid we can find him in the objects of our daily experience.

CHAPTER XI

WE have considered universals and particulars. We have seen them to be no self-subsistent or even distinct facts. Our ideas about them are arrived at by abstraction from a nature that is a whole and is individual and concrete. All their inferential derivatives, such as causes, atoms, electrons, and ends, on the one hand, and the irreducible residua of feeling and sensation, on the other, are likewise found to be abstract ideals, when sought for as actual entities. But they are abstractions appropriate at levels in which reflection is active, and are ideas required for the interpretation of the real. Mind itself, but only again by abstraction, can be presented for science as what has developed into what it is through evolution in time and space. That abstract conception of mind as a pure phenomenon leaves over another question, *to* what it is that evolution and the world which it implies present themselves. It is only *for* mind that they are there, and as the consequence of this the mind, which is the objective existence to be accounted for by evolution, has been postulated as already actually present in the world in which the evolution takes place which is to account for it.

How is this difficulty to be got rid of? Only by giving up the notion that mind is merely an object in our world existent at a single level in knowledge, something, too, of which experience is an attitude or property. What we are forced to do is to turn to experience itself, and to see whether in our experience of mind it has aspects other than that of a mere object among others. It has this last aspect, but that need not be the only aspect which it presents. It may be subject as well as object, and these may be inseparable, save in an artificial disseverance which hides their real nature.

What is our experience? In it both universality and particularity are implied as moments. Actual experience consists neither only in quantities nor only in feeling divested of all generality. As we saw, this is true even of here-ness and now-ness. They are general conceptions present in what is actual, but in what as being actual implies the presence of characters that belong to what is universal.

Experience always involves reference to an " I " which stands for subject in the experience The " I " thus involved is, taken by itself, no part of its own object-world. Such an " I " is presupposed by the world within which alone evolution takes place, and therefore evolution cannot account for it. The idea even of myself as sitting in a chair writing postulates the subject *for* which this very idea is present. Such a subject is no more, when we have excluded by abstraction its particularism, than what thought always requires as the centre for its activity. The " I " is in this way of the nature of a universal, inasmuch as it is the form, not merely of experience of a particular object, but of the activity of reflection which, entering into the constitution of experience of every kind, makes it actual. Of myself as pure subject I can form no *picture* at all. For my images are always descriptive of an object confronting my mind, not the less that presentation to subject is implied, and that the self which is the foundation of the object-world and the condition of its reality cannot subsist by itself as object. It is by conceptions arrived at by reflection, conceptions that are necessarily general, that we define the " I." " I see what I am writing." This experience implies reference to a subject which is not itself definable in terms of the experience which it only

renders possible, and apart from which it
is not perceived as actual. It is through
divergences in particular experiences that I
distinguish myself as known in experience
from the selves of others as similarly known,
and find myself free to make mistakes.
Everyone says " I," and in so doing everyone
expresses a universal which is not merely
resembling but is identical in all individual
knowledge. The distinction of individualities
numerically implies space and time, and
these involve and depend on an object-world.
When we merely say " I " we have not
logically got to space and time. Reflection
carries us further than it is sometimes taken
to do.

On the other hand it is beside the point
to talk of an absolute as a separate and
definite entity to be assumed in this connection. All we can do, here as earlier, is
to point out that in the individual form of
all reality the universal is as much implied
as is the mere particular, and that neither
is actual apart from the other. It is to the
meaning of individuality, with levels at
which it discloses itself, that we are thus
again brought back in a question that is
concerned with the root of reality.

The actual is our experience, and our
experience is the actual, with its implication

of general and particular as moments in involving each other. We start from experience. We cannot directly get behind it. All constructions, such as the space-time continuum, relations and their terms, the categories and ideals, are discriminated out of experience as having their basis in it. It appears that experience is always an active process. Its nature is to appear in degrees and at levels, and so to point to an ideal and depend on a character that is essentially self-developing.

Now this is no mere metaphysical hypothesis. It seems to be what observation and the reflection which observation requires disclose. What is stated is what characterises all experience, æsthetic, religious, and scientific. Experience cannot be resolved into mere fixed terms and relations. These are what they are only as determined in abstract conceptions fashioned by the mind. The same criticism applies to all attempts to display it as point-events on the one hand, or universals on the other. It is no " complexus of intelligible relations." It is attempts of this kind that have led to the sharp opposition between the standpoints of realism and idealism. But if the actual is neither universal nor particular, but is an individual that implies both in its constitution, there is no room for this sharp opposition any more than there is for ruling out the larger ideal which is involved. The supposed antithesis seems to arise out of views which are too abstract. Science and metaphysics are apt to live not only in ignorance but in contempt of each other. Yet both are necessary in criticism if we are to get rid of our prejudices.

CHAPTER XII

MAN AND GOD

WE have seen how mind not only moulds the object-world of nature but itself appears as an object there. We have also seen how in the activity of mind, as the essential significance of the self of which we are conscious, there discloses itself a universe within, that inner universe of which Goethe wrote. These two phases of the universe do not signify distinct facts. They fall within a single entirety. In its fullness this cannot appear to us in mere pictorial form. We interpret it as a single whole, but we do not, even in abstract reflection, ever completely grasp it in the full phases of its detail, notwithstanding that the principles which underlie reflection know no barrier to their might. For they are forms in which we generalise, and it is as such that the conditions of our station in nature open them to reflection. Art and religion bring us nearer to them at their proper levels in the actual facts, but in the shapes of symbols that are no more than symbols, incapable of giving us the real adequately in individual shape. That is at least partly because human intelligence in its activity finds limits in the organic conditions under which it is expressed in the object-world. The universe is for us fuller and higher than the universe for a dog, but we can conceive a view of that universe just as much fuller and higher than ours is above that of the dog.

What art and religion do is what abstract thought as such cannot accomplish. They bring before us, in ideals fashioned through reflection, individual experience, transformed and raised in interpretation to higher degrees than those of the other objects on which the mind naturally fixes. The power of mind outstrips the activity which is present in perception, and so develops it for mind that our experience takes place at levels that are above those of daily life. Such experience, like all other, is individual in form. The particularism of feeling is implied in every phase of existence. But the transforming power of the mind makes its object symbolise and become expressive of conceptions which lift it. It is the character of mind with the limitless freedom that is its foundation which brings this about. Mind alone has this lifting power. Through the conceptions which the objects of art and religion symbolise what it has fashioned

in higher order is freed from what binds it
to ordinary immediacy.

We human beings experience our world
through our senses. It is a felt and seen
world in imagination as well as for direct
perception. The organism can know only
under this condition. Even when its aspect
is that of being intelligent it is bound up
with the limitations imposed on perception
by the brain and nervous system. But
these are still expressions in bodily form of
intelligence and are its instruments. They
bring about the entry into experience of its
particularism. But they are mind itself in
a form that not the less is that of mind,
because it assumes for us the aspect of an
external object in nature.

Thought enters unlimitedly into all perception. As with the physicists in the case
of time and space, we are always discovering
more and more how it moulds the object.
Yet the process is for us inexhaustible. The
residuary aspect of feeling eludes complete
reduction. Still, in theory, for us mind is
intelligible as delivered from what presses
itself on men, the unending separation of
general from particular.

Just as in theory we can sum up a series
with an infinity of terms, so in theory we
can conceive mind as raised above this

separation. Mind so conceived must not be treated as if confronted by any object foreign to itself. Its object must be itself and it must find itself in and as its object. The separation between subject and object is progressively superseded and the universe without becomes one with the universe within, the single whole into which all that is, was, and can be, falls. Such a universe we cannot present to ourselves as an image. For what is imaged is dependent on feeling, and feeling belongs to mind expressing itself through the senses. But none the less such a universe can be the true interpretation of the ultimate character of our experience. If we use the word " absolute " in this connection it is well to remember that the expression, if attempted to be exhibited in detail, has in the history of thought invariably broken down. It has broken down because it has always come to suggest what is really relative, either something revealed not by inference but by feeling, or else a systematic construction by thought which has proved itself to be beyond human capacity to compass adequately, undeflected by insufficient definitions. Metaphors, with their images of individual character, are not enough. We seem to be confronted with an ideal that for us, conditioned as we are, must remain an ideal. But it is an ideal of great potency, which enters into all knowledge and is for all reality the background. In such a form the structure of knowledge requires and postulates an absolute.

It is just in its operating as such a background that the reality of this ideal consists. It is implied in our experience, which always stretches towards infinity. We are compelled by the activity of reflection to be seeking for ever larger wholes, and to conceive of the ultimate whole as such that, though we cannot envisage it, all else falls within it. The story of philosophy in its most diverging forms is the story of this striving. Whether we call it the Infinite, or the Absolute, or God, the ideal is present, if to be regarded as unattainable in imagination. But to regard it as thus unattainable is not to destroy it. If we cannot envisage the foundation of an experience we can tell what it is not, and so, rising beyond mere sensuous metaphors, attain to notional grasp of it. The external universe it cannot be, for that is clearly relative to thought. Nor is it an internal universe in the sense of being what is confronted by a not-itself. It is the entirety which reaches over both. Its nature must be of the nature of mind, because mind alone reaches over and includes both aspects

of the universe. Yet because we are forced
to fashion symbols even when we reflect
in abstractions as the mathematician does,
we have always to watch our symbols and
to see that the thought of which they are
the expressions does not become inadequate.
Close criticism of the categories we use is
not less desirable here than elsewhere.

For what we mean by God we must thus
primarily look within ourselves and not to
what is without us. Less than all-embracing
mind God cannot be ; mind, too, that knows
no foreignness in its object, and is not limited
by an inexhaustible particularism. Such an
all-embracing reality is conceivable at least
in reflection. The particular has no existence
excepting as disappearing within knowledge
to an extent that is limitless. Taken by
itself it has neither meaning nor reality.
We must not image to ourselves mind at its
highest level as either confined to abstractions or as sentient. The two phases arise
from a distinction which falls within it. Art
and religion have symbols in which this
truth is told to us. These symbols express
for us directly because metaphorically the
universals which fashion them, just as the
marks in algebra convey the meaning they
stand for. In themselves they are not adequate, but they point us towards conceptions

that would be adequate if they were capable
of expression in our human language.

God cannot mean less than the universe.
But this does not signify the point of view
of the pantheist. God is mind, mind that
manifesting itself in us embraces a universe
that is more than one of matter and energy,
a universe of spirit that in us has rest, and
fashions all that is for us within and without.
That is the explanation of why the world,
despite a contingency which is the outcome
of limitations in our experience, is ultimately
rational. That is also why we have faith
in the harmony of experience, and can rely
on it as a basis for our faith in the working
out in the long run of probabilities. God
so conceived is closer to us than breathing,
nearer than hands or feet. Yet define him
in language that does not mislead we cannot.
Such definitions are always in the end pictorial. It is only with what we sometimes
call the eye of faith, the realisation of things
unseen, that we can behold God, but religion
and art alike tell us that such faith can
sustain us.

CHAPTER XIII

LEVELS IN KNOWLEDGE AND REALITY

WHEN I consider my world I find that I have experience of the most various kinds. I see, to recur to a previous illustration, a familiar friend approaching. What interests me most is his identity, and the qualities attaching themselves to it. His past, his present, and his future alike enter into his personality. He is continuously changing, physically and mentally, and yet he remains identically the individual person I know. Now this identity is not material identity, for the stuff of my friend's body and his appearance are always altering. Nor does it lie in sameness of behaviour, for my friend's mode and manner have changed as his surroundings have changed. His knowledge and his moral qualities are to-day different from what they were when we first knew each other. The actual identity of John Smith is one which has persisted despite continuous change. It has required unbroken evolution to render it what it is. The identity is of the character of what is understood rather than of what is directly perceived. Apart from the particular circumstances and conduct of John Smith it has no meaning, but on the other hand it gives significance to his circumstances and conduct. His personality is not a mechanism, nor a mere life, nor a psychological construction. It is mind expressing itself in the object-world, but as mind. That mind should present itself as an object is, a fact which experience makes manifest. The portrait painter daily demonstrates this possibility. Even our own minds we recognise as embodied. Had I a bad headache or were I drunk I should find myself in part deprived of both capacity and mental freedom. The Behaviourist School in psychology takes a view that appears to be too restricted. But at least it has shown how much of what we call mental bodily movement is capable of expressing. Mind thus objective is really mind. We may not be able to find a sufficient expression of the self-creating activity that distinguishes mind through mere sense perception of the living human being whom we know. It is obvious, too, that the dissection of a dead brain in the laboratory is the dissection of what is dead and is not the same thing as study of the conduct of the living. But our human personality involves a living body as well as a soul, and our knowledge embraces all of the orders or levels in which these are made manifest.

What is the soul ? Not an entity apart. Not an *animula, blandula, vagula* ! It is rather that in a man's personality which the expression of his face and his free action express ; the form to which all the rest is as matter ; the organism at a higher level in the actual world. The personality of him who is speaking to me depends on more than can be rendered in relations of time and space ; on more also than on mere life. It belongs primarily to what is intellectual and ethical, and has other qualities that are qualities of the spirit only. That seems to be the nature of the soul, the personality as expressed in bodily form. It appears in an aspect which belongs to time and space. Yet it is no more the creature of time and space than is knowledge itself. The doctrine of degrees and levels in reality appears to render intelligible experience that without it would involve dilemmas.

That doctrine delivers knowledge from being confined to the exclusive and single aspects which would limit its activity to the interpretation of relations in external order in time and space. Knowledge does not admit of being expressed exhaustively in these relations ; they are *for* it and enter into the object-world from which it seeks to distinguish its activity. That is why the rendering of mind into an assemblage or succession of point-events has always broken down when tested by epistemological scrutiny. The truth, here as elsewhere, is the whole, and the whole includes the subject as well as the object aspect, not as separate existences, but as aspects separable out of the entirety in reflection only.

With personality we are in a region where what concerns us is what distinguishes humanity from the merely animal as well as from the merely mechanical. The three aspects do not exist as facts side by side and independent of each other. They are different presentations of facts in experience, not reducible to each other, but requiring for their description different conceptions and different language. The good, the beautiful, and the true are ideas that illustrate the field of discourse that belongs to this higher region. We see them and their contrasts expressed in the faces of our fellow human beings. They are no doubt in a measure dependent for their maintenance on the bodily condition. But this condition does not explain or create them. They belong to a level in knowledge beyond that at which a merely living organism is presented.

Yet without a body the soul, which is its form at a higher level of knowledge, could not be there. It is to this extent conditioned by the body, and by station in nature at which mind is object for mind. The processes of the brain are requisite for the activity of intelligence. Physiology plays a large part in the modern science of psychology.

That knowledge has levels at which its forms are different is no *a priori* deduction. It seems rather to be a fact of which we have constantly to take cognisance in observation. The rabbit, the horse, the elephant, and the ape all display intelligence of degrees which are short of what is human in normal cases. The respective ranges of conception, with the resulting limitations in " universe of discourse," are apparent to the observer. When we bring ourselves back to the starting-point, which is our individual experience of the object-world of nature as an entirety, it ceases to be perplexing why knowledge should be thus graded. What confronts us in that experience is a world in space and time which is developing itself. Mind appears in that object-world and is recognised as to some extent symbolised in temporal and spatial forms. These are not adequate for its full expression, but they enable its partial expression in ways that show us that it is

mind that is there in the behaviour of the
men and animals we see. It is so that we
find before us mind that has an object
aspect. But we are ourselves more than
mere objects in this world of nature. We
experience it, and the particularism of that
experience is fact only in virtue of the
universals of knowledge. It is on the character of these universals that the grading of
experience into levels depends. The " be-
haviourism " of the intelligent factors in
the object-world enables us to classify and
define the conceptions that enter into their
mental activities and their worlds. These
activities extend to what we call mere instinct in one direction, and to human intelligence in another. But for their comprehension and for their very presentation in
knowledge our minds have to be more than
they appear when merely observed in their
settings in nature. The entire universe belongs to the object-world which is *for* the
subject, and the subject reaches in reflection
over it. The subject taken by itself we can
reach, not perceptually but only notionally,
by abstraction from nature. It is a logical
aspect of the actual which has no significance
apart from it. Only by reasoning, based
on the fashion in which we are conscious of
the dynamic and developing quality of know-

ledge when it expands its implications, do
we reach its character as essential in the
actual. When we observe the self in its
object form, as it confronts us in nature, we
find it primarily invested with the attributes
of time and space. It appears as a history
or sequence of events in the world. That is
how people, ignoring the other phases which
what they are aware of presents, come to
think that it can be resolved into successions
and assemblages of point-events. When they
think so they are considering experience
only under one of many aspects, all of which
are essential. As has been seen, the various
aspects under which the real presents itself
to us are not subjective qualifications which
the mind imposes on something which exists
independently of it in another form. The
various phases of the object-world do not
conflict, because they are the outcome of
different standpoints with different categories. But these are all objective in the
sense that they enter into the character of
the actual and make it what it is. Life is
as real as mechanism, and intelligence is as
real as life. The beautiful and the good
and the divine enter into and fashion the
constitution of our experience of the world.
When we do not find them it is because the
standpoint of our knowledge does not include

the conceptions which are required to recognise them as actual. That is why, if we
knew all, we should find the whole universe
revealed in the flower in the crannied wall.
But, fashioned as our minds are, they require
to proceed by ignoring what they are not
searching for and to employ methods and
outlooks which do not admit of the whole
nature of the real being taken in at a glance.
That, too, is the reason why our metaphors,
mere images as they are, never appear
adequate.

CHAPTER XIV

KNOWLEDGE AND ITS LEVELS

WE have seen how we are driven to a conception, fuller than we ordinarily bring to bear of ourselves. In what is different from Professor Dewey's conception, and is more nearly analogous to Kant's synthetic activity of intelligence, we find what transcends the separation of personalities, and indicates a universe that includes both what is within and what is without the mind. That which is all-embracing and is creative is in us. But not as a separate entity. The nature of ultimate reality is that of our experience raised in reflection to a degree that supersedes the separation of its object from itself, of the particularism of sense from the generality which characterises thinking. That experience is, in the aspect in which the might of thought can render it, the self, but the self as an ideal one towards which the highest forms of reflection can only impel us, conditioned as we are in brain and organism. We cannot truly describe it even in symbols, for these are restricted by their sensuous nature, and can only suggest and not be adequately envisaged.

Still reflection even of this order knows no barrier to its range of activity. It can free the range of thought to an extent which has no limit, if it cannot exhaustively define. The self, delivered from distortion by metaphor, we find it difficult to describe in everyday language. Yet some definition is possible. Despite the hindrances referred to knowledge ought to prove to be sufficient for its task. Were it not so the self would have no final reality, for it would have no final meaning.

Sufficient knowledge of ultimate reality is, however, knowledge of a kind different from that of any object of perception. It has obviously to be at a level at which the distinction of mind from its object does not obtain, and at which what reflection points to is an entirety within which all that is, the particular as well as the universal, falls. It is therefore knowledge through conceptions of an order such that human beings do not employ them in their everyday practical classifications of experience.

That there are orders in knowledge through which its kinds are distinguished, we have seen. Such orders may bring us to larger conceptions than those which we deem

adequate for ordinary use. This is so not
only in philosophy but also, for example,
in the severest mathematical physics. One
of the greatest of contemporary mathematicians, Hermann Weyl, concludes the
mathematical investigation in his book on
Space, Time, and Matter with a passage that
is worth referring to :

" The laws of the metrical field deal less
with reality itself than with the shadow-like
extended medium that serves as a link
between material things, and with the formal
constitution of this medium that gives it
the power of transmitting effects. Statistical
physics, through the quantum theory, has
already reached a deeper stratum of reality
than is accessible to field physics ; yet the
problem of matter is still wrapped in deepest
gloom. But even if we recognise the limited
range of field physics, we must gratefully
acknowledge the insight to which it has
helped us. Whoever looks back over the
ground that has been traversed, leading
from the Euclidean metrical structure to
the mobile metrical field which depends on
matter, and which includes the field phenomena of gravitation and electromagnetism ;
whoever endeavours to get a complete survey
of what could be represented only successively
and fitted into an articulate manifold, must

be overwhelmed by a feeling of freedom won. The mind has cast off the fetters which have held it captive. He must feel transfused with the conviction that reason is not only a human, a too human, makeshift in the struggle for existence, but that, in spite of all disappointments and errors, it is yet able to follow the intelligence which has planned the world, and that the consciousness of each one of us is the centre at which the One Light and Life of Truth comprehends itself in phenomena. Our ears have caught a few of the fundamental chords from that harmony of the spheres of which Pythagoras and Kepler once dreamed."

This passage suggests that the roads of approach to the nature of the real converge. It is in all cases a question of how we can examine our categories sufficiently critically. It is evident that experience cannot, if it is to be fully understood, be divorced from the intelligence for which it is experience. Knowledge is in the deepest sense foundational for reality. Mind and its object are in the end inseparable. The symbols which the mathematician requires are images not the less that they are pregnant with his interpretation. Object requires subject, and together they enter into the individual form which is that of the actual.

To get further light on experience we must therefore again turn to the nature of knowledge. Its nature is capable of being exhibited in the domain of logic and it is identically present in minds that know, even through their divergences. For truth and error are the outcome of freedom under those organic conditions through which alone knowledge is possible for us men. It is thus conditioned though not created by our station in nature, as the outcome in those aspects of the self that belong to nature through a process of evolution. Freedom is that of a finite self when it reflects. But evolution takes place in an object-world which has meaning only as there for mind, whether perceptual or conceptual. Now if we look at the nature of knowledge as it displays itself in consciousness we find that it is of different kinds. The experience of the mathematician is different from that of the biologist. The first gives meaning to his world through ideas of order in externality. The second gives such meaning through ideas of behaviour, not under the influence of causes, external in time and space to their effects, but in realisation of ends which operate apart from consciousness as immediately present ; not at any distance however indefinitely small, but directly.

That is what our observation seems to tell us, and bio-chemistry, if properly assigned to its own level, does not detract from the testimony. It is the power of the end as realising itself that seems to account for the uniformity of the myriad descendants of a minute organism, and for their inheritance of common forms and qualities. The kind of interpretation is for the mathematician and the biologist radically different in each case. The immediate influence of ends in moulding the modes of behaviour which we recognise as life cannot be expressed in differential or other equations. As reality depends on meaning, the meanings being different the aspects realised are in their truth different.

But the two kinds of interpretation do not come into collision. They belong to different orders of reflection and of what is actual. The organism is indeed subject to the laws of cause and effect and of the conservation of energy. It has aspects in which these dominate it. But they are not the aspects which make it an organism. The latter aspects, when presented and isolated by abstraction from the concrete actuality, are what they are in virtue of the conceptions which are foundational to the kind of experience with which we are confronted. The mode of observation depends on the kind of knowledge that our direct experience requires us to bring to bear, and this again depends on the conceptions that control in these kinds of knowledge.

Conceptions enter not only into knowledge but into its objects. It is by their significance that objects exist for us. That is why the latter as exhibited in reality always express and embody conceptions. But objects thus displaying themselves in different orders are not necessarily on that account and in that fashion numerically distinct. The constituent substances of living organisms may be investigated chemically. My friend whom I meet in the street is so many pounds weight of carbon, nitrogen, oxygen, hydrogen, etc. He is also a living organism, embodying the features of life and of ends realising themselves, and preserving functions which remain his normals through life and through continuous changes in material. But it is the same object that appears under the two aspects. Again this very object is perceived by me who encounter it in the street, as a self, as another " I " numerically different from myself in so far as it occupies a different station in space and time and has a different history and content as an object of nature. But my friend is more than a living organism that may have this separate existence. He is at a different level an organism with another aspect, that of human personality. As a person he is distinguished by me from myself, not only by his different place and appearance in nature, but by a mental history moulded by these differences. Still he and I think in large measure identically. We have notions which are logically the same, and not merely resembling as objects in space may resemble. Each of us is for himself " I," and in that way each of us recognises the other as " I." If we did not think identically we could have no common world in which we lived. Mind is not a thing, neither is it, in its distinctive nature, a happening in space and time. It is the activity of free knowledge, and as such it has no locality, inasmuch as locality has meaning only as its object. Knowledge is in logic the *prius* to reality, and its form even as moulded by the organism implies that it signifies that it is more than what is so moulded, and is the foundation of that form.

We have now seen that the general conceptions which it employs determine the levels at which knowledge operates, and, as the result, determine the kinds of objects which it fashions. It is through conceptions of a higher order than those of mere life that I perceive and interpret the friend whom I meet in the street as being, like myself, a person. Mind appears for both of us as in the world. But it requires for such appearance a different order of conceptions from those of mechanical or even merely living things. Once realise that perception involves conception and this can readily be grasped. It follows that knowledge must have a variety of levels with their counterparts in the experience that depends on it.

The approach to the interpretation of what men mean by God is now less hard. The conceptions which we use when we contemplate the objective world are not enough. For they are applicable only in individual forms which entail sensuous aspects. Of these we cannot wholly rid ourselves, dependent on an organism with senses as we are, however far we may carry the unending process of subordinating them. The symbols used are therefore inadequate to the ultimate truth, even when employed in art and religion at their highest.

Yet the might of thought is such that it can carry us beyond these symbolic representations to a reflective view of the universe as a whole in which the foundation is mind that in thinking its object creates it. Such mind is super-personal compared with mind as we experience it. It makes no severance of its object from itself or of itself from its object. Time and space and all order in externality must fall within it, together with the other orders in experience. In the entirety they have their places, but these places as gradations in order of reflection and not as separate entities. The truth is for us in this sense, here as elsewhere, in no perfect form, but it points us to an ideal and perfect whole, which we may regard as absolute.

On this whole our human knowledge rests for its foundation and source. In human personality the final order is revealed, but revealed in object form and from a station and period in nature. The human soul is thus imperfect. But because it finds God in itself it finds also in the human self an expression of his infinity.

These things are there, even in the external world, for the intelligence that is wide enough to apprehend the levels that they express. And the distinction between knowing and being appears therefore to be in the end only relative and not final.

CHAPTER XV

SOUL AND BODY

IT will be appropriate to add a little more at this further stage about the relation of the soul to the body. The soul has obviously a close relation to the body. It cannot be a separate " thing," nor does it act externally or causally, in the strict sense, on the latter. Nor, on the other hand, is it as soul wholly detached from it, as though it were purely of the order of a subject, in knowledge. For it is an object included in our experience, and belongs to an individual and concrete world. We come back to the view that reality presents a variety of aspects, and that the soul must be, as ordinary experience indicates, the organism in an aspect different from that of the mere organic body. That does not mean that the organism produces it, as a piano produces a tune. There the relation of causation obtains. But it does mean that what we popularly call the body possesses aspects in which in the course of our experience it proves to be more than an organism, and that in experience these aspects are just as real as any others. It is the doctrine of levels or degrees in reality and knowledge alike which helps us over the difficulty.

If the soul is the body in a higher aspect we shall expect to find that the soul increases in perfection with the quality of the body. And this is just what we do find. A beetle has an organism of a low character, so low that we can perceive little or nothing which we can call soul. For the soul properly so-called is presented as an object that seems in its nature to be akin to mind. It is not in itself mind, for the characteristic of mind is to be knowledge. A dog comes nearer to being a soul than does a beetle. For he is intelligent, and appears to possess some reasoning power and freedom in con-scious choice of what he does. He shows the presence of a self in a nascent form, for he recognises his kennel as his own and is capable of jealousy. He has even stan-dards of conduct, at the breach of which he is sometimes ashamed. He also may show unmistakably disinterested affection for his master.

But the organism of man is of a yet higher order. In the development of the brain, in the varieties in his individuality and in consequent departures from what is con-ventional in his species, in his erect and commanding figure, in his power of using his hands ; in all these and other qualities his organism is of a higher type than that of any lower animal. The brain of man is capable of neural processes so intricate and minute and so different from each other that it is obviously fitted to express qualities which are unattainable by the mere brute. Apart from these qualities the human soul could not be. For it seems to stand for their expression in a new light and from a new standpoint. The living body regarded from this standpoint is the manifestation of a human soul.

No doubt the soul may properly be said to consist in feeling and reflection, and the power of basing on these consciously directed action. The neurones of the brute are suffi-cient to be the vehicle of movement and of life based on feeling and consciousness, and of intelligence up to a certain degree. But the nervous system of the brute cannot take him higher, into the ranges which are those required by human intelligence alone. It is man's body that is requisite for the ex-pression of man's intellectual and moral nature, and that nature is limited by his body. An injury to the brain may destroy his mental capacity or interfere with the possibility of its expression. An affection of the brain may produce chronic depression in the bravest. We human beings are conditioned by the kind of senses we possess, and the soul of an angel, if there be such, may be found to have other senses and a range greater than ours. For the soul appears to have no separate locality and to be nothing detachable from the living organism. It seems rather to be just the organism interpreted at a level above that of mere physiology, the level of life as the expression of mind.

In mind we are subject which recognises itself as having the whole universe potentially present to it, not as a merely external object but as falling within itself. Without the unifying quality of the subject, which is requisite to make knowledge possible, there could be no time or space. For it is only for the subject, that is as falling within knowledge, that these have any meaning. When we see our neighbours acting in a way that implies that they are of our own level and think freely as we do, and call themselves " I," we speak of them as persons, meaning that they are the expressions of what is not in itself merely a happening in outside nature, but imports intelligence that is, in what is fundamental, identical with our own, excepting in the details of the symbols

which are used to express it. In no other
way can we reach the intelligence of our
fellow-men excepting by recognising our very
inmost selves as in them too. Mind is
conscious of them and so *finds* itself. The
circumstances of the living human being, his
history, the contents of his personality, may
all vary from our own in an infinity of details.
But the cardinal quality is that he speaks
and behaves as an " I," just like we do.
This quality is no effect caused by experience,
for it is the very condition which lies at the
root of an experience such as is ours, and
that makes it possible. It is its logical
condition. To a limited extent it may be
present in the dog. But not as the " I "
which lies at the root of human personality
and of its higher manifestations in intellectual
and ethical life.

The soul thus appears to mean the body
interpreted as at a level at which it is much
more than a merely living body. In the
soul we have risen above that degree in
completeness which is all of which nature is
capable. It is better described as what
Aristotle called the " Entelechy " of the
body—the end, in the true sense of the word,
which determines its behaviour and is expressed in that behaviour. We cannot express it merely in terms of feeling, nor is it

any mere set of universals. It is concretely individual in that both feeling and the reflection which defines and sets feeling enter into it.

If the body passes away by decay or death, the soul as such in its object form therefore passes with it. But that is for mind only a passing of reality at a level belonging to the object-world. The " I " *for* which alone the object-world is present is not a happening which can pass in the same fashion. A man can contemplate his own pain and his own death, and can regard them as events not touching his higher nature. That does not mean that he will put on some other body when he dies. It means that his personality exists at a higher level than does his object nature, and is not within the reach of external causes. If he dies he may cease to be as a person an object for the bystanders. But his ceasing to be such is an event which, so far as he is concerned, is an event from which it is of the nature of his mind to be detached. The " I " was not born and does not die. For it is not and never was an event in the time and space which belong only to the forms in which it manifests itself. Mind is above nature. It is of a different order in conception, and at a level at which birth and death have not the significance they possess as physical events. In the case of the animal that has not full personality this will not be so.

These considerations do not help us towards the ordinary pictorial representations of a future life. Such representations are of a soul, with some new kind of body. But they give to the faith which triumphs over death a rational basis. For they point to the world as passing away only as before a mind that is not itself in time or space.

CHAPTER XVI

HUMAN PERSONALITY

To conclude that our personalities to a large extent mould our experience, even when we are dealing with personality in its human form, and apart from degrees in knowledge of a higher order which seem implied in it, is not an extravagant conclusion. For relativity which we find in our experience of the self implies an ideal in the light of which this relativity becomes apparent in ordinary life. To discuss this ideal, and to try to render it sufficiently in terms that at best must be abstract and general, may not prove easy. What we can do most surely is to indicate where the conventional view of everyday life seems to fall short, judged by the necessary tests.

To begin with, the hard-and-fast separation between subject and object is found to be everywhere deposed from its authority. That does not mean that there is no distinction between them, but rather that the distinction is not a final one. Such separations, in cases which present suggestive analogies, are being broken down wholesale in the progress of the latest science. Time and space are no longer treated as separate entities or as independent of the observer. The relativity without limit of space-time systems is looked on as, at the very least, a possibility of which account must be taken. We assume a particular system as real when, regarding the earth as at rest, we see the sun going round it. We realise that an observer on Mars, who based his space-time system on Mars treated as at rest or even as in motion round the sun, would have to measure operations on the earth very differently from an observer on the earth who was treating himself, in the way our observers do, as at rest on the earth. We have to devise a special standard for measuring the true velocity and proper time of a Beta ray. In cases such as these everyday knowledge is obviously only relative, and is inadequate to a final rendering of the actual. Modern teaching about relativity in physics has introduced this principle in a new form intermediate between the everyday view and that of metaphysics.

So it is with the distinction between subject and object generally. The more closely we scrutinise our knowledge of the object, even in our most apparently direct perception of it, the more do we find that reflection has entered into and transformed it, and that the object is for us inseparable from the subject in experience. Categories are required, and standards of value, not only for the interpretation of what we think we perceive immediately, but for the attribution of reality to it. The spiritual does not exist for a dog, and probably not even the variations of fine colour. For ourselves we have before us a world that seems at first sight to be independent of us and always the same. But it turns out, as we have already seen, to be what it is only because mankind always brings to its interpretation a common set and level of ideas which give fixity to experience.

It is impossible to draw a line that can be treated as final between the object-world and even the human mind for which it is there. As we scrutinise closely more and more that object-world turns out to be rendered in universals and to belong to reflection. If we say that these universals belong to the object-world and are somehow inherent in it, like particular facts, that does not help us. The only meaning we can attach to such a statement is that mind enters into the constitution of the object-world, and that the distinction between the two is consequently obliterated.

Mind ceases to be regarded as merely included in its world, for mind seems to reach over that world, and to absorb it progressively the further we study the process of the over-reaching. Here as elsewhere our difficulties arise from metaphors which we apply " dogmatically," that is, without first considering whether they are legitimate in the subject-matter. For in experience we do not appear to find the sharp demarcation of independent entities which such metaphors seem to assume. At one stage in the structure of the knowledge we apply such metaphors may be natural and proper. But it does not follow that they are equally legitimate at another stage. We may talk of causes when we are at the level of physics and chemistry. But it does not follow that we may use the images of these when we are inquiring into the control of ends in bringing about the behaviour of living organisms, or into the relation of motives to the exercise of volition.

Human personality thus moulds its object-world and gives it forms which the minds of animals do not give to it. But human personality is itself moulded, though in a different fashion, and so moulded that its everyday interpretation of its world seems to fall as much below the truth as in another fashion does the interpretation of the animal. For beyond our personal standards there are intrinsic in the constitution of the mind of man phases which are relatively speaking

super-personal. There is an objectivity in
our knowledge, truth that is truth for everyone, which does not vary with the individual
and which we do not challenge. That is
what we mean by the real. Then there
are " values " which we do not challenge.
They are for us " critical," we cannot go
beyond them. We can render in their terms,
but we are unable to resolve them. The
fashion of the day may pass, but in that
fashion there has been a standard that is
invariant, depending on more than what is
transitory. The history of thought, since
the time of the Greeks, of the Platonic Idea
and the Aristotelian " Active Reason," has
been mainly illustrative either of this super-
personal phase in mind or of a challenge of
the mere forms in which it has been expressed,
rather than of controversy about the underlying substance of the doctrine. Among the
metaphysicians of to-day there is observable
an almost constitutional aversion to speaking
of an " absolute " or of universals as existing
in the object-world independently of reflection. But there is a corresponding aversion
to the heresy of mere individualism and of
solipsism. We have studied Kant, and we
may think that he went too far in his attempt
to treat the activity of thought as separable
from its material in his theory of experience.

But beauty itself was really looked on even by Kant as a form of truth, and so was value.

These things illustrate the faith that the self is more than it commonly regards itself as being. It is certainly more than merely a passively contemplative intelligence enclosed in an animal body. Such an intelligence could not be, even in a limited sense, a centre of its world. It would encounter more limits than the higher animal encounters.

The self is in this sense super-personal, not in being dominated by another and different self of a higher order, but in, as it stands, displaying orders of knowledge and reality alike in which it tends to pass beyond the limits within which a consistently conventional standpoint would confine it. We are hampered by the physical and physiological configuration which mind assumes in our experience of it. But that experience is only intelligible if its foundation is taken into account. Were we only what the bodily self suggests to us we could hardly escape from solipsism. We do escape from it as soon as we recognise that even our own knowledge is dependent for its possibility on being not so limited. Beyond the range of our senses we cannot reach directly. But the mind is not so hemmed in. It can recognise itself as identically present in other

selves, and discourse not merely about a
world but about a universe. That is because
inherent in its very nature is its transcendence
of its physical level and the conceptions
which are fashioned at that level. We find
this in beauty ; we find it in values and in
our faith in the good, and in the difference
between right and wrong ; we find it in our
consciousness of the divine as a fact of life.
But we find it most clearly in knowledge
itself. In that transcendence of common
orders in knowledge which we call genius
it confronts us, but we do not need to resort
to genius in order to witness the higher orders
in mind. We witness them in the advances'
of knowledge, and in its penetrating power.
Knowledge reaches far over the immediate
and goes beyond it. It exhibits the phenomena which confront us as illustrating
principles which transcend ordinary measurement, and go beyond order in externality ;
principles which reduce space and time to what
is relative to the observer, and which carry us
back into our minds as the source of what
we have taken to be of fixed order in nature.

The advances of modern knowledge seem
increasingly to be breaking down the sharp
line of demarcation which we took to exist
between nature and even the particular mind
that observes it.

CHAPTER XVII

THE STRUCTURE OF EXPERIENCE

WE have arrived at a stage where the view now expressed should be further contrasted with that of Professor Dewey. For him experience is in ultimate analysis a self-contained entity, existing as prior to knowledge which finds in it its genesis. In the course of experience so conceived knowledge is regarded as being evolved. It is for him in other words a product causally produced by experience, with the field of which it is not in fact conterminous.

The view of this book is that experience in separation from knowledge is a notion arrived at by mere abstraction, and when sought to be taken by itself is wholly unreal. Knowledge turns out to be foundational to the actual. But not foundational to it as a cause operating *ab extra*. For the two are one within an entirety, and are divorced in it only through artificial processes of reflection. Mind, in the degrees and at the levels in which it is found as an object in experience, presents itself as an object in nature. But as so presented it does not offer to us the whole truth about itself. It is always potentially more than it appears at particular levels of its object forms. It points us to a larger view of itself in which the whole object-world within which evolution operates is relative, and is what it is only *for* mind. Mind in the form of object only in a qualified way discloses itself as subject for which the world is, but not the less the level of the subject is implicit even in the object-form in which we perceive and recognise it. We saw this when we found that in the neighbour whom we meet in the street we recognise the " I," as subject in knowing, just as much as we ourselves are. Not only are he and we both " I," but it is in logically identical knowledge that our objective world is actual. Without such identity there can be no common world. Subjects in such knowledge have as such no meaning as numerically separate things, and the particularity of station in nature does not imply that they have. Such apparent particularity only shows how impossible it is to dissever experience from our knowledge of it, and to regard experience as disclosing only isolated orders of reality. It is because of the fundamental identity of our knowledge of things that there is an objective universe. That is what was meant when it was said long ago that in knowledge there is in truth only a single subject. It is within the universe that is intelligible as there only for the subject that is identical and single that all physical and biological and ethical processes take place. If every phenomenon in such an objective universe were interpreted through the same conceptions, if these conceptions had not the diversity of the different orders in knowledge to which they belong, the world could not be the rich concrete world it is, or hang together. But reality appears at different degrees, turning on the form of the activity of knowledge concerned in fashioning it. These degrees constitute among themselves a hierarchy, and the higher the conceptions that belong to its stages the more nearly do we approach to what we may call mind as fully constitutive of reality. The activity of our individual knowledge may be never so much conditioned by our stations in nature. Not the less does it always increasingly develop the recognition of reflection as entering into reality, the more searchingly it is scrutinised. It is the principle of levels or degrees in knowledge and reality alike that delivers us from difficulties in interpretation which we could not otherwise overcome. It is this principle that also points to the breaking down of the apparent demarcation of the actual from our reflection on it. It indicates, too, the separation of the particulars of sense from the universals of thought as tending to a vanishing point and superseded in a final whole.

Knowledge is thus foundational. It signifies more than in daily practice we attribute to particular minds. For within it particular characteristics fall as its objects, isolated within the whole by the conceptions which our station in nature drives us to bring to bear. But these conceptions neither stand still nor are complete in themselves. They have their functions within the orders to which they belong, and these orders fall within the general system of knowledge.

Such an idea is not new. It is the idea to which not only some of the most prominent thinkers of the ancient world, but some of the foremost among the successors of Kant, have tended, an idea which in varying shapes they sought to elaborate. In the result, as it was for them and is for us, idealism and realism become no more than counter-abstractions. For what is experienced and knowledge are not two but one.

If this idea be a true one, then knowledge and experience or nature are of course not separable entities. Experience takes its form

from knowledge as expressing itself in it.
That knowledge has levels ; it is of different
orders. These enter into experience and
are the keys to its various forms. It is not
separable from the reflective grades which
render it what it is for us. They are not
always before our minds in it. For these
minds themselves appear in nature and are
experienced as conditioned by it in that
appearance. They are indeed always more
than they seem to be, for the more fully
they are comprehended the more do they
disclose their foundation in that subject-
aspect which as minds they possess. But
they never appear as mere fixed things. Although before knowledge as its objects they
have knowledge for their inherent nature.
John Smith is a self, an " I," with a world
before him which is for mind identically the
world that is before me, subject only to such
diversities as his different conditions and
station in nature, as a citizen, as colour-blind,
as deformed or dying, give rise to. It is in
the higher orders in which our common
experience realises itself, that the identity
lies, an identity that is characteristic of
knowledge as such. We are together in the
world and yet in a deeper sense not of it.

The orders in knowledge are apparent.
In its rudimentary aspects we distinguish

events as exclusive of each other in space and in time. These distinctions may not be the simplest conceivable. But they are distinctions within knowledge in primary forms of order, distinctions which are yet intelligible only for a mind in which the events are held together in such relations that they form a whole of a kind. As we have seen we come simultaneously to higher and less simple orders which enter into our experience, and without which it would have little meaning for us. Why they are before us we do not ask. They belong to the foundation of knowledge. In its inherent character they must have their origins, for we cannot reduce those that are of a higher order to those that are of a lower. They seem to be implied in the very character of thought as revealed in experience, and to be no more capable of explanation by anything beyond than is knowledge itself. For knowledge is the condition of all such explanation and is itself foundational. It does not lie outside experience, nor is it a product of experience. Experience, past, present, and future, belongs to and is for and falls within it. That circumstance does not detract from the necessity of exploring a world that cannot be deduced. But it does warn us against plunging into dubious metaphysical assumptions which treat knowledge as something other than foundational. There is not experience and then knowledge. Knowledge and experience are inseparable in their unity. It is a unity which we really assume from the outset, and on the basis of which all inquiry is founded.

Such a view of the nature of reality is not without certain analogies to that of Professor Dewey. In both views the starting-point is experience, the actual. In both the process of advance is an unravelling of the character of nature. But difference comes in early. Knowledge, the realisation of the meanings which nature discloses as we pass from mere causes to ends, is for him a latest word, a phase of experience which it evolves as the result of interactions which are dynamic and its characteristic. Nature is there for him, not through the medium of knowledge, as falling within it, but independently of a result to which it has itself given rise. For us this cannot be the case. Experience, even in its primary forms, is always knowledge of some kind and falls within and arises through it. No doubt experience appears in diverging orders. By our abstractions we treat these as though they were the distinguishing characteristics of different things, belonging to different kinds.

Mechanism and life and beauty seem to us to exist exclusively of each other in so far as we do not accept the standpoint from which they appear only as different grades at which the objective world discloses itself in the mind which has it for its object. But these orders and their manifestation in different phases of our experience do not coexist or succeed or interfere with each other. They belong to levels which are logically different, and are not interpretable as interfering with or as reducible to each other.

For mind that was free to experience and construe its world *sub specie æternitatis* the different orders might be a perfect and complete hierarchy, constituting an entirety that was not split up into degrees even apparently divergent. Matter and mind would in that case cease to be antithetical. The moment of the particular in perception would dissolve altogether and disappear from reflection, because the unending series in which the process of knowing takes place for minds that are precluded by natural conditions from taking in the whole, would have been completely summed. Mind of this order is what our experience never fully discloses to us. And yet it is an ideal we employ in our knowledge, and more than an ideal. For we assume its reality as the foundation on which alone knowledge can rest, and on which alone its orders are explicable. Attempts have been made repeatedly in the course of the history of philosophy to determine deductively and in full detail the character of mind of this absolute type. They have failed one after the other. The reason is that we human beings always have to think in individual images, even when we seek to think most abstractly. We thus turn our absolute into a relative, or a set of relatives, according to the phases we attribute to it. But this difficulty does not stand in the way of our recognition of mind of a higher order than experience presents as being the necessary foundation of such experience, and of knowledge as being not only ideally but in truth an entirety. Such a recognition is sufficient to deliver us from difficulties that seem otherwise insuperable, and it is enough to allow reality to what we regard as highest in our lives. For it provides not only for necessary developments of thought, but for values, in ethics, in art, in religion, that seem to have their foundation in higher orders of mind.

We saw that it was only as the expression of knowledge and of the experience that it contains that our neighbours as we met them in the street were real for us. But neither they nor we are real as things of which knowledge is the property or product. Knowledge is rather the essential condition of all existence. It expresses itself in ourselves in orders and at levels of different natures. What we have to do is to recognise that these do not interfere with each other. What is a mere thing at one degree of knowledge and reality may be a self, a subject for experience, at another degree. Since it is of our essence to be mind we are free to accept as the expression of what is actual our experience at the level at which it is our object. In so doing we can rise in our standpoint, and realise that for knowledge that is ideally complete it is only the whole that can be the truth.

CHAPTER XVIII

MAN AND DEATH

WE are born and as an event required by the course of life we die. For experience shows us to be objects in that world of nature where we have a time and a station and a period of growth and decay. But we have seen that we are more than this. We are subjects in knowledge and persons, and our personality implies that as such we are not the creatures of time and space, and that our knowledge has levels that are above those where mechanism and life are the forms of the world. As persons we are subjects, ideally the single subject for which not only mechanism and life but higher degrees in reality, which still admit of distinction between personalities, find meaning. What is our world? It is one which includes beauty, goodness, the divine, and truth. Such a world is there for the mind which it confronts, and the line of demarcation between mind and that world is a disappearing one, for philosophy and for science alike. Knowledge and reality are in final analysis inseparable. To know and to be are phases that fall within a larger entirety. The universe within and the universe without constitute a single universe.

If this be so death is obviously an event, but not an event with the vast significance which it has as one of the facts in nature. Beyond doubt it has great significance from the standpoint of nature as we directly apprehend it, the standpoint of our station there. It brings loss and sorrow and may, after its fashion, mean disaster. But these concern the individual organism that feels and knows, and has a place in the family and in society. They do not reach to the meaning of death for the individual mind that suffers it. For that mind death indeed is an event. The body may cease to live and so to fulfil any further function in the external world. But that ceasing is itself a happening in time and space, for the mind that experiences its own death. Such an event is like birth, a natural part of the course of life. Unaware of a self before birth we may be without perceptual awareness of a self after death. For dying is a process in the object-world, a happening which we present to ourselves. It does not follow that we go on contemplating it after the death which has come to us. Nor have we need to do so. Time and space are forms of that object-world which seem to necessitate for their apprehension the continuance of the organism. But at all periods of the world's history man has found it possible in thought and in resolution, by the exercise of a more penetrating insight, to triumph over death, even in the very act of dying. He has proved himself to be a mind able to treat the termination of his life as a mere occurrence which does not touch what he holds to be highest. He has a standpoint from which death has no sting and the grave has no victory. The inner universe absorbs into itself the outer. It is not hard to see what this means from the outlook to which the problem with which we have been dealing presents itself.

As subject the individual seems to be beyond the reach of the termination as well as the commencement of its consciousness of its world, for that world, and the consciousness of it also, fall within what is there only for the subject. In this respect death is in some respects like sleep. Sleep belongs to the object-world of happenings which are before the mind in its experience. So does death. That we do not awake from it in the same way makes it not the less a happening which we can contemplate as one that is no more than an occurrence in our object-world. The time and space in which it takes place are relations with meaning only in reflection. At a higher level of contemplation these relations do not affect the knowledge for which alone they are there. The activity of the self has transcended them. They are not merely felt. They are known. For the observer, who observes under the forms of time and space, the organism of the dying man ceases to be sentient and to live. But there is a yet higher level in the knowledge of him who contemplates his own death, at which that death is not abolished but superseded, just as the self supersedes itself in great impersonal action, such as dying to save another or to save the nation, the dying which is metaphorically called dying to live. In such cases the future of the self ceases to be of concern. The reason is that the level of the spirit reaches beyond such concern, for it is a level that is timeless and spaceless. We have seen that the highest form of knowledge is implied in our finite apprehension as constituting the essential foundation requisite for its explanation. In the highest kind of knowledge the factor of the particular must be conceived as not merely indefinitely resoluble, but as completely resolved. It is not, as in merely perceptual consciousness, a limit which thought cannot reach, but is ideally an aspect which is absorbed into individuality of a fuller order, the individuality in which object and subject are no longer differentiated, but in which to think is to create. That is not all. The character of thought itself alters. It no longer consists in universals distinguished from particulars which are of a nature limiting to itself and for that reason never finally resoluble. Mind and its object must, at such a higher level, fall into unity. The progress of science and of metaphysics alike represent a continuous advance towards such an ideal condition. The difference between knowing and being is always tending to disappear as analysis becomes increasingly penetrating.

With this progress towards resolution of apparent self-subsistence of events apart from mind, the self-subsistence of the event of death becomes resolved with it. That is why in poetry, in religion, and in action, in each of which the higher forms of thinking are revealed in similes or in metaphors, death is treated as transcended and ceases to be of more than a vanishing importance. We can never in our earthly lives rise above our "that," the station and period in the world of nature that our individuality implies. But we can so rise above it in our thinking that it may cease to concern us at the higher level that we are conscious of even in an earthly existence which is inherently at a level other than that of such concern.

It is not by setting up a fresh picture of another bodily life at the end of this one, to be continued in time and space, that we reach or can maintain this level. It is rather by making ours the higher significance of such metaphors as that life eternal consists in doing the will of our Father that is in Heaven. His Heaven is no other world. It is just this world comprehended and accepted as what it finally and really means. Subject and object are no longer thought of as dissevered. Reflection transcends the disseverance. We are indeed more than we take ourselves to be, even as we pass from among the friends who are grouped around us.

CHAPTER XIX

THE OUTCOME

By way of conclusion we may now sum up this review of the character of our experience.

The factors of the general and the particular in our experience have been assigned to their places. They are no more than aspects of a whole that alone is real, and within it they fall and are separable only in reflection. The mind of man has its expression in a living organism with a period and station in nature. Physical science and biology, with the various forms which the principle of development assumes in the latter, account for this period and station, and for the limitation of our mental capacities. They belong to the aspects of man's existence in which it is an object for perception, in an external world, and to this aspect they are confined. But the doctrine of levels or degrees alike in knowledge and reality shows that man is more than merely an object for himself and others. He is indeed the outcome of a process of evolution, but he is not less subject. We say " subject " and not " a subject." The reason is that the

pluralism of individualities belongs primarily
to the region of time and space, and these
are relations having their origin within the
world of objects. They owe their character
to the nature of the knowledge *for* which
that world is, and which gives it its meaning.
That we have a world before us, that in addition we all apprehend and contemplate it
in the main identically, implies that knowledge is more than a mere property of a
particular object called the brain. The
brain is the expression for us of human
intelligence, but in another aspect it is a mere
thing which the anatomist and even the
physiologist have to envisage in abstract
form. The dead brain on the dissecting
table means existence at a lower level than
the living brain in which feeling and intelligence are expressed.

Even in the object-world we see it is
obvious that reality exists at different levels.
That object-world is actual only in so far
as it has meaning, and its meanings are of
different orders. The order of meaning of
the living and intelligent brain is higher
than that of the dead brain lying on the
dissecting table. Even the living brain with
the functions with which the psychologist
concerns himself is, like this, an object in
nature, studied in conceptions which shut

out higher orders in mind, such as beauty and truth, presented in our human experience. If we would get at that experience in its fullness we dare not shut out these higher orders, higher because more akin to the actual character of mind, for they enter into that experience just as much as do the other and quite different orders belonging to the relations of externality. These higher orders are, in the abstractions which our freedom enables us to make, sometimes disregarded and at times not even present potentially to intelligence of a limited nature. Our dog runs along with us on our walks. But he is not cognisant of the qualities of the scenery. He distracts us from our meditations and he is a kindly and intimate companion. But the higher orders of knowledge are not present to him. Nor are they invariably apparent in the minds of the men and women who also walk with us. To take in the full meaning of life is not everyone's business. And yet unless it is taken in we have no approach even to a complete consciousness of what life means for mankind.

The life of man implies for the completion of its meaning that no phase of reality should be excluded. We are all in some measure specialists. But in our particular specialism we have always to recognise that there are other possible forms of concentration on what is best. We fail, so far, if we are oblivious to religion. We may not think its metaphors sufficient to make it reliable in giving exact knowledge. But they are metaphors which imply conceptions of a high order, and, even when we cannot look on such metaphors as sufficient, we ought to regard them as expressing, in the way that is most readily accessible to religiously-minded people, phases belonging to the full nature of our minds of which religion is in possession, the truth that there is a level at which we rise over pleasures and feelings that are passing and come near to what is the real foundation of our existence. So it is in music and in poetry. Even if in their technique they do not appeal to us personally we may find in them what lifts the soul above the transience that is characteristic of nature. " Die Gestalt," said Goethe, " dieser Welt vergeht, und Ich möchte mich nur mit dem beschäftigen was bleibende Verhältnisse sind."

The world of our experience manifests itself not only in scientific orders but in forms which point symbolically to the presence of other orders, orders apart from which mind is not free to realise itself in its completeness. It is not only philosophy that lifts us beyond ourselves, and dispels the foreign and menacing aspect that the external world and death present. An experience which displays itself, not only in abstract universals but in our knowledge of it as possessing different grades and degrees of reality that vary, will display these grades and degrees in an infinite variety of ways, all of which may be actual and true of their kinds. That fact does not derogate in the slightest from the necessity of logical and scientific method or throw doubt upon its necessity. What it does demand is that we should be watchful about the categories we employ in our reasoning about the phenomena we observe. Provided that the categories we employ are appropriate, the strictest methods, both of induction and of deduction, are not only open to us but are necessary. But if we apply conceptions with which we think ourselves familiar uncritically of their appropriateness to the kind of objects we are observing, we get into troubles in our reasoning about which Kant warned us long ago. Knowledge, for example, as even introspection discloses it, is not made up of sets of successive series of impressions which can be exhibited as a simple time and space relation of objects external to each other. Mere association is no principle that explains

it. For knowledge is that through and in
which such association takes place and becomes possible. Do not let us, then, take it
to be sufficiently explained as the spatial and
temporal association of the ideas which are
its objects. Such a method seems to mean
that knowledge is being brought under a
conception that does not fit it. The result
is inevitable failure to grasp what it implies.
The universe rests on a foundation of a wider
nature than this. To the understanding of
that nature we are not helped by methods
based on the analogy of those in mathematical physics, confined as these and the
conceptions employed by them are to bare
order in externality. Moreover, the symbols
in which the sciences are compelled to express
the conceptions they employ are but abstract
symbols, inadequate for other phases of the
rich world to the interpretation of which in
various fashions they are directed.

We need not then disturb ourselves when
we find in poetry and religion statements
made which are lacking in this kind of precision. For it is not such precision we are
in search of when we turn to them. What
we seek is to have our minds lifted towards
the consciousness of new meanings in what is
actual, meanings that can only be expressed
in pictures of individual form, but which

not the less direct us towards the kind of truth we are in search of. That from other standpoints we must be critical of these pictures does not therefore destroy their value for us. The universe is a whole and the truths which it yields to reflection are of different kinds.

It is of interest to illustrate this principle by reference to its neglect in theology, as much as in the sciences of nature. In current literature some examples of the distorting effects of this neglect are given.

In his strenuously written book *Lourdes*, Emile Zola tells the story of the cure at Lourdes of the heroine, Marie Guersaint. The majority of the Paris physicians who had seen her had diagnosed a lesion of the marrow, believed to be the result of an accident. They thought the case hopeless, but raised no objection to her being taken to Lourdes. It could do no harm. But another Parisian doctor, who had also seen Marie, took a different view. Like his colleagues he had no faith in the miraculous interpretation by the Church of the processes at the Grotto there. But he differed from their diagnosis. He was of opinion that the case was one of no more than auto-suggestion, brought about by the violent shock of pain produced by an accident. If a sudden and sufficient determination could be induced in the patient to throw off the false idea of physical pain and paralysis, bringing about a will to breathe freely, and suffer no more, then a cure would at once take place. What was essential was the lash of an intense emotion. He therefore not only advised that Marie, who was very religious and capable of intense belief, should be taken to Lourdes, but predicted that if she was, and the emotional conditions were satisfied, she would recover. A devoted Abbé Pierre and her father escorted her on her journey. She suffered much but became full of faith. At the Grotto, in the midst of a crowd stirred to intense emotion by the priests who addressed it, she suddenly rose and declared, what turned out to be the case, that she was completely cured. The Abbé Pierre, who knew of the dissentient diagnosis, unfortunately indeed for his own peace of mind, could not bring himself to regard the cure as miraculous. It was psychological and it had turned out exactly as the doctor had predicted. The mental bond was broken, but broken by a cause of which science could take account, and which fell within ordinary laws of nature.

Now this story of Zola's is an illustration suggesting how easy it is to misconstrue the

field of experience by the application to
phenomena belonging to one order in it of
conceptions belonging to quite a different
one. The ecclesiastical authorities at
Lourdes had recorded a miracle as the
cause where it seemed unnecessary to suppose that there was any miracle at all,
or more than what was due to suggestion.
A wide enough view of the phenomena of
life would have found what occurred to
belong to the sequence of these phenomena.
But the priests at Lourdes had introduced
in religious metaphors mechanical ideals of
a cause which not only was outside that
order, but was in conflict with it and therefore supernatural. Had they simply insisted on the meaning of religious faith and
on its power over the mind, they would have
had no need to introduce the idea of a non-
natural cause, the direct interference by a
physical act of the Virgin with the bodily
condition of the patient. But apparently
they fell into a paralogism, and into a mistake both of logic and of fact.

This kind of paralogism is an example of
what mankind is highly prone to fall into.
People concentrate on a phase in an experience that is of more than one kind, and construe the phenomena which belong to that
phase with the aid of ideas that belong to

other and distinct phases. We always tend towards mechanistic notions because they are the simplest, and belong to that domain of time and space as frameworks of the not-self which seems to confront and be independent of us. To turn to causes external to the events we meet with is thus natural, even in the metaphorical reasoning of religion, and we search for such causes in every field of experience, regardless of the question whether it is a field where the idea of externality applies. Even where such ideas are excluded by being superseded, as at times in poetry and in some of the language of the Bible, we find metaphor and simile with some physical reference breaking in ; such is the tendency of the unrestrained imagination. But these break in only to come into conflict with the facts and interpretations of exact science. This seeks to confine itself to what is yielded by observation conducted on definite principles appropriate to its own domain. It does not always succeed. Just as poetry and religion stray into its own field, so it strays into other fields, and seeks to treat all facts observed merely mechanically or biologically. Those who wield the instrument of criticism have always to be watchful. The appropriate categories are selected naturally and objectively if we keep in mind the character of knowledge. It is not separated inherently from reality by any gulf. The nature of reality is to be individual and our categories enter as much into the objects we apprehend as they do into knowledge itself. We err because mind is free. But the ideal before us in the character of knowledge as a system and entirety is our guide to that truth which is the ideal whole and nothing short of the whole.

Such must be our attitude to the experience which is always the actual. The might of thought, thought which extends into observation and experience and not less into the compelling recognition of quality, wrests from the experience which confronts it the details of its structure. But just because our knowledge is a system it is a system which must contain, if it is to be adequate, all of the conceptions which may have to be brought to bear if account is to be taken of the full range of the actual. We are finite, that is to say we are minds manifesting themselves as having stations in nature in which they are conditioned by the nervous structure and the organs of sense in which these minds express themselves in nature. But they express themselves as mind, and it is of the nature of mind to be free even when it is finite. To the range of our reflection

there is no limit set so long as the life of mind
in nature endures. And even when so
immersed in nature the mind is yet free to
know. We have seen that it is at every turn
more than it takes itself to be, and that it
can trace the relativity of its own knowledge
to the conditions by which its life and activity are affected.

We need not therefore dismiss as of necessity wholly without reality any phase in our
experience which confronts us as apparently
actual. It is one thing to discover that we
are interpreting any such phase through
conceptions that do not belong to it, and that
bring it into a false context in reflection. It
is quite another thing to deny its reality, a
reality which may be of compelling power,
merely because we have not before us the
conceptions which are alone appropriate to
the presentation of its proper place in our
reflection. These, when we have ascertained
them, may seem to separate the sphere for
us of the phase we encounter from the spheres
of other phases. The orders in knowledge
may be so different that the orders in reality
are hard for our reflection to bring into
relation. But that is no justification for
failing to regard experience as a whole, or
for denying that it has many aspects, each
possessing the significance that is peculiar

to it. Bare relation of order in externality ; mechanism and causation ; the immediate results of ends in unconsciously determining behaviour in the sphere of life ; consciously purposive action ; freedom in volition ; the compelling claim to recognition of degrees in quality : these are illustrations of what we find when we regard the entire field of our experience. They point to a hierarchy of categories which enter into the individual character of the objects of experience. In that hierarchy each sort of conception has its application and its level, and the levels are distinguished by us as belonging to an ideal entirety which gives their character as rational to knowledge and reality alike. In the end, and despite the contingency which is everywhere, in the externality confronting the individual mind that has before it a world that is outside itself, the universe seems therefore rational. Indeed, at every turn we have to assume that it is so. Without such an assumption we should have no assurance of that belief in the ultimate uniformity of nature on which all our knowledge, including science itself, rests. Only on this assumption do we reject the miraculous when it claims to be the intrusion of some order of conceptions into a field to which it is not on the face of that field appropriate. Only

on this assumption do we base our belief
in the principle on which the calculation of
probability rests.

A poem descriptive of the death of a deeply
religious man describes in detail his severance from the world in which he has lived.
That world becomes for him a series of events
which pass away, and the relativity of his
knowledge of it becomes apparent to him :

> So much I know, not knowing how I know,
> That the vast universe where I have dwelt
> Is quitting me, or I am quitting it.
> Or I or it is rushing on the wings
> Of light or lightning on an onward course.
> And we e'en now are million miles apart.
> Yet—is this peremptory severance
> Wrought out in lengthening measurements of space,
> Which grow and multiply by speed and time ?
> Or am I traversing infinity
> By endless subdivision, hurrying back
> From finite towards infinitesimal,
> Thus dying out of the expansive world ?

There is the account of what may be a phase
in the experience of the saint. But the
sense of the beauty in it is individual and
cannot be rendered into terms of knowledge
in metaphors that apply only to the external
world. And accordingly, in the "Dream of
Gerontius," as the poem goes on to describe
the ascent of the soul of the dying man into
the presence of God, we feel how even John

Henry Newman lapses into descriptive ideas which have no true application to the region before him. They are metaphors, belonging properly to another level of human experience, and are no more than symbolical. And yet they are symbolical of a phase of experience that is real. For they indicate the sense of a triumph of the spirit over death and the grave, a triumph that is not the less actual because it is only one of the spirit. These things belong to a real experience, an experience which we put from us because of its inconsistency with science only in so far as it arrays itself in descriptions of external fact in metaphors which in truth distort the description by claiming for it a validity of a scientific nature which is alien to its own nature.

It is not necessary for the argument here to go further, and to seek to exhibit as a systematic whole set out in detail the categories and orders which enter into experience. In the course of the history of thought the attempt to do this has been made. But in our time it is not likely to be made again with general acceptance. The attempt at such a systematic arrangement of notions is too likely to become involved in error due to subjective influences, to be looked on as reliable. It may not be an attempt that it is beyond the power of thought to make and accomplish. Such is the range even of thought as we find it that its might must, in theory at least, stretch even to this. But the effort does not appear to be a profitable one. An Absolute so reached invariably tends to become a pictorial absolute, and is as such no more than what is relative. For it is only in images that we can think at all.

But the ideal of mind finding its object as fully one with itself is an ideal which forces itself upon us. In this way we postulate what is absolute, and we have to do so. It must be present, for its truth is assumed as the basis on which we judge our world to be rational notwithstanding the appearance of that contingency which fuller knowledge is ever dispelling. Experience has, as we have seen, many orders, and each of these is inherent in reality because it is inherent in knowledge. In our actual experience we distinguish these in their differences of quality and range. They emerge for us in the form of general knowledge which only our abstractions divorce from the individuality which they have fashioned. That individuality in being actual is concrete. It is never inert and it has many phases all of which present themselves in accord with the categories we really find in them. Our difficulty in accepting their reality is, not that they are not present to us, but that by a false application of conceptions that are foreign to them we treat them as though they belonged to levels that are not their own. It is so that we get into difficulties that are wholly unnecessary. It is not the reality that is lacking but the proper way of reflection on it.

Two courses are open to the man who would live the fullest and highest life. One is the way of philosophy. He has there to study and examine critically the conceptions he employs when he reflects. He must disentangle and set in their proper places in his mind the categories that seem to enter into what he holds himself to be directly aware of. But philosophy is a difficult study which requires a lifetime.

The other is a simpler course ; the acceptance of the inherent reality of what is higher, as much as of that which is lower. This way does not require philosophy. It is an act of belief in the reality of faith akin to, if not much the same as, our faith in the external world. For the " beautiful soul " God is present and by that soul his presence is practised. There is no theory. There is rather an avoidance of theory. Neither a particular creed nor abstract knowledge is required. What is implied is only the acceptance of experience as truly including many phases, and among them those which lay claim to values that seem the highest. But the alternative courses which may be pursued are not in all respects mutually exclusive. The sense of religion and of beauty may shade into desire for a philosophy, or philosophy may seek what is concrete and individual in aid of its systems. Plato, Spinoza, Kant, Goethe, Wordsworth, Thomas à Kempis, illustrate how phases that are different may be closely related to each other. For, in the knowledge that has grasped its own nature, truth and beauty, the divine and the human seem to find their harmony. It was Carlyle, in no conventional sense a Christian, who, recalling his own father, tells us that he himself, by manifold struggles, came to feel his feet on the Everlasting Rock, and through time with its death in some degree to see into eternity with its life.

THE END